The
GOOD LUCK
Cat

The GOOD LUCK *Cat*

How a Cat
Saved a Family,
and a Family
Saved a Cat

Lissa Warren

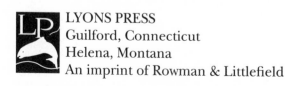

LYONS PRESS
Guilford, Connecticut
Helena, Montana
An imprint of Rowman & Littlefield

For my parents, of course.
And for the cat beside me while I wrote this.

CONTENTS

THE WALTZ ON THE RED-BRICK PATIO

And the brown-eyed boy who asks a dance
is the low bough on the buckeye tree
and his hand in yours is a broad new leaf
and his fingers thin as branches.
If you listen close you can hear the roots
push their backs against the mortar
and the dappled bricks are almost warm
in the light of almost-summer.
And it may seem like you're wasting time
but this is what you do
when you're ten in Ohio on a Sunday afternoon
and everyone you've ever loved is living.

—LISSA WARREN
(originally published in *Oxford Magazine*)

Chapter One

Homecoming

*Let a man get up and say, Behold, this is the truth, and
instantly I perceive a sandy cat filching a piece of fish in
the background. Look, you have forgotten the cat, I say.*
—Virginia Woolf

In Thailand, it means good luck. Si-Sawat—the good luck
cat, the Korat, the Blue Siamese. Always given, never sold.
Gifted in pairs to newlyweds and people of high esteem. One
of the oldest—and purest—of breeds. Trained, in ancient
days, to check a crib for scorpions (no mere mouser, the
Korat). Carried on elephants into battle by Thai warriors.
First mentioned in the manuscript *Cat-Book Poems*, written

in 1300s Siam and currently housed in Bangkok's National Library. A "national treasure," by government decree. So beloved by King Rama V that he ordered state funerals when his favorites died.

But their history, while rich, pales in comparison to their appearance: eyes the color of a lotus leaf, lavender paw pads, fur as sleek and gray as a dolphin—silver, even, in certain light. And, oh, the personality: vocal and stubborn, smart as a whip, intensely loyal. Right for us.

Here on Stillwater Pond, more than eight thousand miles from Thailand, a cat is a lifetime commitment, not unlike a marriage. In my family, adopting a cat is like adopting a child—not something to be taken lightly.

In 1994, when my father retired from his job as a department store executive, it quickly became apparent that he needed someone to keep him company—to help him pass the time. I'd moved back in with my parents after completing my undergraduate degree (out of choice, not just necessity—I actually liked my parents), and after Dad's quadruple bypass didn't entirely "take" (only the main artery, the mammary one, had bypassed like it was supposed to), I had promised to stay for as long as he needed me. But I worked long hours at a publishing company in Boston, almost an hour's drive from our home in southern New Hampshire. It meant that, in the winter, I barely saw my father during daylight hours. Mom was still employed as a department store executive herself. She sometimes worked fifteen-hour days, preparing for a regional manager's visit, or dealing with new fixtures, or setting up a sale. It left Dad alone more hours than any of us wanted, so my suggestion that we start putting in calls to cat breeders was met with little resistance. The only real question was which breed of cat to adopt.

Our previous cat, Cinnamon, had been a sable Burmese—also Thai, but a bit more common (though she herself was exceptional). Mom and Dad got her for me for Christmas when I was five—had her flown in from a breeder in Texas. She was, and always will be, the best Christmas present I ever received. We were inseparable. She slept in my arms all night, every night, from the day I got her until the day I cried my way to college. She loved me so much that she once caught and killed a chipmunk and dragged it through the house so she could leave it, like in a scene from *The Godfather*, on my bed. Gruesome, to be sure—but in her eyes, a glorious gift.

Cinnamon lived to be nineteen, and her death, from kidney failure, was devastating for all three of us. We were all there when our veterinarian, Dr. Karen Belden, put her to sleep. I was the one who held her, wrapped in her favorite "tiger blanket" with the maize-colored tigress face peering out from the dark brown background. The blanket was soft and warm like she was, and when Dr. Belden went to take her from my arms, I gave her the blanket, too, so she'd have something familiar, even though she was already gone. The folks at Bulger Veterinary Hospital washed the blanket and mailed it back to us a week later, with a condolence card all of them had signed. Perhaps they did that for everyone, but we liked to think they knew Cinnamon was special.

Though we loved the breed, we had had our sable Burmese. There was simply no way we could adopt another one. We looked into other types of Burmese—champagne, lilac, chocolate, cream. But we were afraid that even they would remind us too much of Cinnamon and what—whom—we had lost. It'd be unfair to the new kitten to compare.

Abyssinians seemed like an option. Appearance-wise we liked them, and they were known for their sweet temperaments. They were, however, also known as an "energetic" breed, and I worried that an Abyssinian might be a bit too active for my crossword-loving, novel-reading, baseball-watching father with the three occluded arteries. Bengals, too, seemed like they'd be a handful—though their leopard-like appearance intrigued us to no end. Devon Rex? Too mischievous. Maine Coon? Just too huge. Sphynx? A bit too naked. Himalayan? Awfully fluffy. Russian Blue? Perhaps.

I can't recall how we homed in on the Korat, but I do remember calling breeder after breeder, asking if they had any Korat females who'd be available for adoption soon. I wasn't looking for just *any* Korat female, though. I wanted one who had been born into a loving home and raised by hand—one who would be gentle and not just used to humans, but fond of them. Truth be told, I was also hoping to find a female who was the runt of the litter, as Cinnamon had been. All of us Warrens were small—Dad was five-foot-six, and Mom and I were five-foot-four (if you want to be generous). And, as Dad put it, I weighed "about a buck." At a hundred pounds, a six- or seven-pound cat seemed doable to me. A ten-pounder seemed like a stretch. I couldn't imagine having a tenth of my body weight curled up in my lap. Plus, if she were small, she'd seem more like a Warren.

After many calls and referrals by other breeders, I came in contact with Madeline Lovelace and her husband, Hewitt, of Love Sumalee cattery in High Point, North Carolina. They were highly respected, with a reputation for breeding beautiful, healthy, affectionate Korats. And, as luck would have it, they had a litter of three born on October 27, 1995, with a tiny female named Thai Princess who needed a good home. The name was fitting, as she had royal bloodlines. Two months prior, her father, "Gideon" (official name: Ruangdej), had become the first Korat to be named the International Cat Association's top cat of the year. What's more, she was third-generation Thai. Her great-grandfather, Chiangmai Chup—the grandfather of her mother, Malee Rose, or "Rosie," as they called her—had been imported from Thailand. Imported Korats, we were told, have more documents to prove their country of origin than most humans do.

I would soon learn that this kind of detailed family history is the norm for every Korat. Over the years, a dedicated team of Korat enthusiasts has maintained the breed's history by keeping track of each cat's lineage through census forms that they send to owners and breeders on an annual basis. And of course they also keep track of how various Korats fare in competition. These records date back to the first time the Korat competed for championship honors, at an American Cat Association show in King of Prussia, Pennsylvania, in June of 1966.

After a careful vetting process that included myriad questions about our house and our experience with cats, as well as our thoughts about indoor versus outdoor cats (they were glad to hear we were staunchly indoor), Madeline and Hewitt mailed me two pictures—one of the three kittens alone and one of Rosie nursing her brood. There was also a note telling me which kitten was to be ours: the petite one in the back.

Ours.

We almost didn't get her, though. By the time I arrived in Secaucus, New Jersey, on March 24, 1996, to pick her up at the agreed-upon meeting place—the Penn Jersey Cat

Club show—Madeline was having second thoughts. Unbeknownst to me, she and Hewitt, just for kicks, had shown the kitten that morning, before I'd gotten there, and to their surprise she had won ribbons. *Several* ribbons. Whatever imperfections they saw in her—a slight banding in the coat, a little kink in the tail—the judges must have missed.

Madeline informed me of their wish to keep her, despite the fact that we'd had a deal and I'd driven all that way. But Hewitt, seeing my face fall when she delivered the news, promptly picked up Thai Princess and put her in my arms. I bent my head down to the kitten and she gave my nose a quick but definitive lick. She had claimed me—even Madeline could see it. This cat was a Warren.

I handed over the $800 check—no small sum for a recent college grad working at a literary press (my parents offered to chip in, but it was important to me that she be a gift)—and the Lovelaces handed me a gray (of course) folder that contained a carefully maintained copy of the kitten's family tree. In her spot, they wrote in the words TING-PEI, the name Mom, Dad, and I had chosen for her. At the time we didn't know anyone of Thai descent, so, with no one to ask, we did the best we could. It sounded vaguely Asian to us and, as dopey as it may seem, we wanted to honor her heritage somehow. "Princess" didn't sound very Buddhist to us and, besides, we weren't the type of family that would have a cat with a cutesy name.

Then I signed the adoption papers in which I promised not to breed her with anything other than another Korat of traceable ancestry, not to sell her or give her away without the breeder's knowledge and consent, and not to have her declawed. With that, the Lovelaces gave me her favorite kitty bed—a plush, red, donut-shaped jobbie—and sent me on my way, with hugs and their best wishes.

Ting slept in my lap the whole ride home, and Mom and Dad were at the front door waiting when we got there.

CHAPTER TWO

The Littlest Warren

*"But I don't want to go among mad people," Alice
remarked. "Oh, you can't help that," said the cat. "We're
all mad here."*

—LEWIS CARROLL

Exhausted from the combination of cat show, car ride, and
homecoming, Ting slept straight through her first night
with us. And her first morning. And much of her first
afternoon. But shortly before dinner she decided to go
exploring—to make our home her home. Unfortunately,
she started with the toilet.

We'll never know what possessed little Ting to go for a swim—whether it was curiosity, poor balance, bad aim, or a combination—but one minute Mom and I were draping the crust over a chicken pot pie, and the next we heard a huge splash coming from the half-bathroom by the kitchen, followed by what can only be described as a death yowl. We went running and Mom got there first, reaching into the bowl just as I plowed into her, unable to stop because I had on socks and we have hardwood floors. We fell, and Ting, who had hooked a desperate paw into the sleeve of Mom's sweater, came with us. Mom whacked the back of her head on the bathroom wall, "Mommy Lissa" (as I had come to be called) whacked the back of her head on her mom's front teeth, and Ting whacked both of us with her now-free scissor-paws in an effort to get the hell out of Dodge as the towel bar came down with a clatter.

"Stop her!" Mom screamed as Dad popped his head out of the bedroom to see what on earth was happening.

"Potty cat!" I screamed as Ting vaulted past him. It was the only phrase I could think of.

By the time Mom and I got up to my parents' room, Ting had already run behind the rocker and started grooming.

"Don't let her lick herself," said Mom. "She could get sick or something."

"Why can't she lick herself?" asked Dad, thoroughly perplexed. We didn't have time to explain. We are germa-phobes, and we had a cat to bathe.

We felt sure there was no way Ting would tolerate being washed in the bathroom sink—it'd be too much like drowning—so I ran downstairs and threw on my bathing suit while Mom started the shower. We reasoned it would feel like rain—a warm, gentle rain. I don't know if you've ever tried to take a shower with a cat, but if you haven't, don't. Two seconds in, I realized it was a big mistake. Three seconds in, Ting did—and used my head as a trampoline to get to the top of the shower stall, where she clung for dear life until Mom pulled her (and several towels) down.

Mom and I spent the next half-hour crouched on the floor in front of the space heater (wisely, Dad had forbid-den us to use the hair dryer), blotting Ting dry with Bounty (cloth towels were out of the question; we liked the cat, but she'd been in the toilet) and soothing her while Dad sat on the edge of his bed, watching us and shaking his head. Mom, determined to take full advantage of the situation, declared a new rule: From now on, the toilet lid had to be put down. Dad called her an opportunist, but knew better than to argue.

Thankfully, Ting seemed no worse for wear and quickly set her sights on her next area of conquest: the big bay win-dow in the living room and its irresistible (custom-made) window shades. Or, rather, its irresistible window shade *cords*, which to her apparently resembled dental floss. She chewed through two before we caught her.

When she circled back to have a go at a third cord, Dad got the bright idea to lure her away with real dental floss instead—a bait and switch that worked especially well because he had, by accident (or not), grabbed the special mint-flavored floss that Mom preferred and he despised. He plopped Ting down on the kitchen table, unrolled about a foot of the stuff, wrapped each end around his pointer fingers, and held it up in front of her. One quick sniff, two tentative licks, and she commenced chomping, angling her chin so that she could get her back left teeth and then her right. A dentist would have been pleased by her form. She kept going until she had severed the floss, at which point Dad unfurled some more.

Unbeknownst to him, Dad had created a monster. In a matter of days, Ting would figure out which bathroom drawer housed the flavored dental floss and would loudly demand a chance to practice good oral hygiene—aka, get a "mint fix"—every time she heard it roll open. Mom tried switching to cinnamon floss, which it turns out is equally tasty to cats. Eventually, Mom resorted to the far less enticing unflavored variety. Eventually, Dad started sneaking off to the drugstore to get Ting the mint kind.

None of this helped the shades, by the way. No sooner had we replaced the two ruined cords than Ting munched her way through a third and a fourth—and later, a fifth and a sixth. Mom, exasperated, put the "blind man" on speed dial. Dad seemed a little . . . proud?

This was pretty much how my adolescence had gone— me doing something of questionable logic, Mom express- ing horror or dismay, and Dad attributing it to "moxie." Take, for example, my attempt at the age of sixteen to go for a midnight swim in Lake Erie with a bunch of my friends—which was lovely, until the police came. Or the beach volleyball tournament I entered on a whim at age eighteen that resulted in a broken pinkie, which kept me from working (at my first "real" job—scooping ice cream at Friendly's) the rest of the summer. Or my decision to get a master's in poetry in an effort to "be more marketable."

It's not that I could do no wrong in my father's eyes. I could, and did, at regular intervals, and when I did, he let me know it—gently at first, but with increasing agitation if I made the mistake again. He was an impatient man—the kind who'd spin around and walk out of McDonald's if the line was more than three people long. By the time I was nine or ten, he pretty much expected me to have my act together. And so, for the most part, I did.

My father didn't have a lot of rules—just a general set of expectations. Be kind until someone takes advantage. Surround yourself with people who default to happy. Work harder than anyone and everyone else. Know how to take a joke but, even more important, know how to tell one. And, for goodness sake, use your head. He didn't care about curfews or allowances or bedtimes, or any of that traditional parenting stuff. He cared about being nice and not being stupid. And he cared about Mom and me.

What few rules Dad did have did not extend to Ting. His patience with her was endless, so he was mostly just amused when, over the course of her first week with us, she proved herself adept at several other forms of redecoration—including the living room sofa which, according to Ting, needed a slightly distressed look, like a pair of jeans from the juniors' department. Little cat, 1; scratching post Dad bought for her, 0. Or the coffee table whose corners, she thought, would look much better rounded—a task she accomplished with a surprisingly minimal amount of surprisingly soundless gnawing. Or the bath mats, which she apparently felt should be changed more often—and which were changed frequently from then on, because she threw up on them at fairly regular intervals after gobbling her food. Or the potted plants, which clearly had entirely too much dirt in them.

In addition to forays in interior design, it turned out Ting was also part tailor. Her specialty: sweaters. Her subspecialty: the destruction thereof. She developed a habit of hurling herself (all five pounds, four ounces of her) at Dad every time he walked in the room, like a little cat grenade—aiming for his chest and occasionally making it. Of course, when she didn't, she was left literally hanging by a thread. He didn't care about the sweaters; he just loved the attention. But Mom soon tired of the mending, and trotted off to Marshalls to buy Dad a polar fleece hoodie—which Ting immediately claimed as a blanket.

We soon learned that Ting was also part rooster, meowing her fool head off at sunrise every morning while perched on the back of the couch—the *bedroom* couch. She didn't get the memo that the Warrens like to sleep late. Nor did she get the memo that ankles are not snacks. Mom's bare legs were simply too much for Ting to resist, especially when said legs were shuffling to the bathroom at, say, five or six in the morning. Mom soon traded in her nightgowns for pajamas. Dad excused Ting's behavior by saying she was acting as his bodyguard. Mom assured Dad that if Ting kept it up and he kept laughing at her while Ting chased her around the bedroom, he'd need one.

My parents had been married for about thirty years by then. They met when they were working at Abraham & Straus department store in Brooklyn, in the flagship location on Fulton Street. Dad was the buyer for infant furniture. Mom was the buyer for intimate apparel, aka lingerie. They shared a stockroom, and figured that because they could manage this without killing each other, they may as well share a life. It wasn't quite as easy as that, of course. It never is. At some point Dad got cold feet and, after much discussion, they broke up.

Then, a couple of years later, Mom came home from church one Sunday to find a note from her roommate saying that some nice guy had called for her, but hadn't left his name. A few hours passed, and he called again; this time, Mom was there to answer. It was my father. They met for dinner that night at Café 72 on East 72nd Street and decided to get back together—this time for good.

In 1968 they were married by a judge in Manhattan, because the Catholic Church couldn't wrap its head around a Catholic woman marrying a Jewish divorcé. A year and a day later, after petitioning the Catholic Church for an exception, they were married in a rectory by a Catholic priest.

When I was growing up, my mother and father were so united that I was in college before it dawned on me that they were actually two separate people. They were in lockstep regarding how to raise me, in complete agreement that I didn't have to "make all gone" at dinner, but did have to take a daily multivitamin; that I should take Spanish in middle school, not French, given the increasing Latino population in the United States; that I was welcome to swear at home, but not at them, and never in public; that I should take theater and dance classes instead of playing sports; that I could stay up as late as I wanted, so long as I was reading. And, of course, that I should be raised with pets.

It has always been about cats for me. Cats and books, books and cats. In my mind the two are inextricably linked, and in college I set about immersing myself in any and all cat-related literature. To this day, I still read and reread poems in which cats play a role. There are the old ones— William Wordsworth's "The Kitten and the Falling Leaves," with "the kitten on the wall, sporting with the leaves that fall"; William Butler Yeats's "The Cat and the Moon," with the cat whose eyes change "from round to crescent, from crescent to round"; and John Keats's "To Mrs. Reynolds's Cat," where he describes its "velvet ears."

But I gravitate toward more contemporary poems about cats—Gerald Stern's "Another Insane Devotion," in which he gives a stray half of his ham sandwich in a gesture of solidarity; William Carlos Williams's one about the cat who steps with such a sense of purpose into an empty flowerpot; Margaret Atwood's "February," with the cat "purring like a washboard"; Carl Sandburg's "Fog" with its "silent haunches" and "little cat feet"; Marge Piercy's "The Cat's Song," in which the cat says, "I will teach you to be still as an egg"; Wislawa Szymborska's "Cat in an Empty Apartment," which will break your heart with its hopeless hope; and Cesare Pavese's "The Cats Will Know," with its "sad smile you smile by yourself." Except, of course, she's not by herself—her cats are all around her.

Short stories, too, have provided opportunities to combine my two loves. My favorite, hands down, is Ernest

Hemingway's "Cat in the Rain," which was supposedly inspired by his first wife, Hadley—his "Paris wife." I became so taken with the story that, the summer after I graduated from college, I took a trip to Key West to visit Hemingway's house—the one with the gardenias and the bright yellow shutters that he lived in with his second wife, Pauline, during the 1930s. Descendants of his cat, Snowball, still roamed the place, and several of them were polydactyl. This made sense given Hemingway's love of sailing. Polydactyl cats had long been thought to bring good luck at sea and, indeed, it was a ship's captain who had given the six-toed white one to Hemingway.

I spent an entire morning with Papa's polydactyl cats beside his saltwater pool, then toured his house where, atop a cabinet in his bedroom, I saw the brightly colored, flat-faced ceramic cat Pablo Picasso had given him. The two of them had become friends in Paris in the 1920s, and Picasso had gifted the statue to Hemingway because he knew how much the author liked cats.

Bibliophile. Ailurophile. I like books and cats. Lovers of the written word do seem naturally drawn to cats. Perhaps it's because reading is a solitary activity but feels less so when a cat's beside you. Not even my favorite books could hold my attention like Ting, though, with her delicate purr and appreciative licks—and propensity for trouble. I don't know what it is about cats that makes people like them better when they're naughty. But they are, most certainly, the biker boyfriend of the animal world: You know you should stay away, but you can't.

Despite all her jobs around the house, Ting did manage to find some leisure time. For example, she learned to use the dresser to get up on the open bedroom door, the kitchen counter to gain access to the top of the refrigerator, and the shelves to reach the pole that ran along the length of my parents' closet. She did not, however, learn how to get *down* from said locations, but she did learn that if she meowed pitifully and ceaselessly, one of us would come find her, turn away from her, hunch over, and let her jump right down. We lost serious back skin to this cat.

Ting also learned to fetch, although she refused to retrieve anything except pipe cleaners coiled like a pig's tail (green ones were a favorite; red, not so much). Her game of choice, however, was pouncing on a piece of butcher's twine as we dragged it across the bed. The game always began with one of us asking her, "Do you want to plaaaaay?"

In her spare time, Ting had taken up studying a foreign language—by which I mean English. In addition to *play*, she knew words like *birdie* (which always made her snap her head toward the window) and *hot stuff* (which sent her running for the bed, certain that towels or clothing fresh from the dryer would soon be piled on top of her which, of course,

they always were—even if it meant we had to throw back in some items that had been washed and dried a week ago).

It was truly an impressive vocabulary. We were not as adept at speaking "cat," but we did start to learn which sounds meant what. Luckily, most of them were some form of "Pick me up," "Pet me," or "Feed me," including the unmistakable "Feed me *now*." Ting drank from the same water glasses we used and ate off the same set of plates— usually not at the same time we were eating, although one of us (Dad) liked to bend that rule.

It should be said that Dad also liked to bend certain rules that applied to *him*. These included eating leftover Halloween candy in the garage when Mom wasn't looking (he'd have pulled it off if it weren't for one stray "fun-size" Mounds wrapper); nibbling Oreos over the kitchen sink while standing in his boxers in the middle of the night (until his heart problem presented itself, Mom used to sneak up right behind him and yell "Jerry!"); weeding without using gloves (the poison ivy gave him away); failing to rinse before recycling (you know you're doing something wrong when the garbagemen reject your trash); and betting the college basketball brackets each March, using not just his name, but mine, Mom's, and even Ting's so that he could enter multiple times. (I bet the guy running the pool at the corner Superette wondered who Ting-Pei Warren was.)

In mere weeks, Ting had adjusted to life with us, and we had adjusted our lives around Ting. We learned which toenails she'd allow us to clip and which ones were off limits, which parts she liked for us to scratch (neck, underarms, and base of the tail) and which were completely unacceptable (belly!). We learned that there's no guilt like the guilt caused by forgetting to take off the house alarm before opening the door to the deck, causing a blaring siren that sent her scurrying under the bed, where she'd remain for hours until we finally managed to coax her out. We learned which hour the shades must be raised for maximum sunbathing time and that the rocker had to be rotated accordingly, that she'd rather be *under* the covers than on them, and that we were done playing fetch with her when and if she said we were done playing fetch with her. We learned that she would "go nappies" about one out of every ten times we asked her to, but that, if left to her own devices, she'd nap a good portion of the day. We learned she'd bite but never break the skin, and that her tongue made an excellent loofah (although moderation was required for the face).

In short, we learned we loved her.

Though we were crazy about her little personality—her spunk, and her smarts—we were, admittedly, also swayed by her beauty. To say she was gray accomplishes nothing. On rainy days she looked cool to the touch, like the shale along Lake Erie, or an old pewter mug. But most of the time she looked more like a shark—solid and saltwater slick. Then the sun would come out, and she'd turn to amethyst in my lap.

Her fur was soft and dense like a chinchilla's, and then there were her eyes. Bright blue at the time of her birth and for several weeks after (we had seen pictures), they had turned to amber during her kittenhood, and we'd been told by the breeder that they would change to a luminous green between the ages of two and four.

Like all cats, Ting was unaware of her beauty, and yet she enjoyed playing beauty parlor—particularly with Mom, who quickly realized that Ting, independent little creature that she was, preferred brushing herself to being brushed. So, after posing the question "Do you want to get bruuuuushed," Mom would just sit there holding the brush—a small white one with plastic bristles that Mom had gotten for free with a Clinique makeup purchase—while Ting repeatedly rubbed the sides of her face against it. If Ting didn't like the angle at which Mom was holding the brush, she'd adjust it by grabbing the brush with her front paws and pulling it closer. To indicate she was done, she'd start gnawing on the brush or thumping it with her back paws. Average session: twenty minutes. I never saw Mom try to end it early.

The Korat is known as "the cat with five hearts." The first is obvious when you look at the cat straight on: It has a heart-shaped face. The second heart is visible when you look down at the top of its head. The third is the heart-shaped nose. The fourth heart is the muscular area of the cat's chest, where the fur comes together in a widow's peak. And of course the fifth is its beating heart.

That heart got a heck of a workout every time Ting had a "nutty." Every week or two, for no reason that we were able to discern, she would take it upon herself to race from room to room, conquering some imaginary obstacle course that involved jumping on the backs of couches, the seats of chairs, the tops of televisions, and basically any other stationary object, including us if we happened to be in her way and standing still. She'd be wide-eyed and puffy-tailed the entire time, the fur on her back bristling, and wouldn't calm down until she had completely worn herself out, which sometimes took several minutes. Even then, her tail would switch back and forth as the adrenaline left her body. Her nutties were disruptive, unsettling, and odd, but we—Dad, especially—couldn't help but appreciate her athleticism.

My dad was not a macho guy. He couldn't do "man" things around the house, like hang a picture frame straight or install a shower curtain rod. He could refill windshield wiper fluid, but that was it when it came to car repairs. When he had a flat he called AAA. Though not a "handy" man, he had been athletic all his life, excelling at basketball despite his size, playing tennis and golf like a country clubber, even though he grew up in the Bronx. He loved Ting for her compact power, which I think reminded him of himself—of the way he used to be.

My father was so proud of Ting, and they were such a perfect match. They just loved spending time together. One of his favorite things to do was to take her for walks outside. To guard against ticks or germs from the wild animals that called our backyard home, he always carried her—tucked her right into his jacket or shirt with just her head showing, so that she could get her fill of sights and fresh air. She never once tried to escape—not even when they came across goslings; not even when they ran smack-dab into our neighbor, Charles, walking Zulu, his hundred-plus-pound (though thankfully mild-mannered) Akita. "Her eyes got big, but she didn't even hiss," said Dad of the encounter. The two of them, Dad and Ting, would walk over the little stone bridge, past the pair of Adirondack chairs by the pond, past the weeping willow where the kingfishers liked to chase each other, and then back across the creek to the house.

Inside and on her own four feet, Ting would follow Dad from room to room. I can't recall ever seeing him climb the stairs to the bedroom without looking to see if she was behind him (which she always was), and then looking to see if Mom and I were watching her follow him. Any good thing, my dad liked to share it.

As a matter of course, we took Ting to be spayed—a completely routine procedure but traumatic for all involved. We were proud, though, to register her as Ting-Pei Warren at the vet's front desk. She was officially part of our family now, and Mom and Dad beamed like the proud parents they were when Dr. Belden called over the other vets to see their first Korat.

So that she couldn't chew her stitches, Dr. Belden sent her home with one of those plastic head cones that attach via a gauze collar. Ting was miserable with it on, pawing at it nonstop and furiously shaking her head back and forth in an attempt to dislodge it. We hated to see her so unhappy—and, truth be told, wondered if all of her thrashing could result in a football player–like concussion—so we untied the cone and slid it off. For the next week we took turns watching her 24/7 to make sure she didn't gnaw at herself.

Some people would call this crazy, but the Warrens were nothing compared to the Egyptians. According to the Greek historian Herodotus, whenever there was a fire, Egyptian men from all over the city would gather to guard it so that cats couldn't run into the flames. Our own devotion paled in comparison.

Herodotus also wrote about how, in Egypt, cats were honored in death just as they were in life—how, when a cat died, its family would go into mourning. They'd even shave their eyebrows as a public sign of their loss, just as they'd do when they lost a human family member.

And of course there was a time when the Egyptians actually worshipped cats—as in, built a religion around them. In the first dynasty there was the goddess Mafdet, "slayer of serpents," who protected sacred places and homes with her woman's body and cheetah's head. And then there was Bast, the goddess of fertility, protector of women and children, and the first cat goddess to actually look like a domesticated cat. All house cats supposedly descended from her, which suggests that our treating them as royalty is entirely appropriate. We spoiled Ting, but at least we weren't erecting temples in her honor.

As the youngest human in the house, I mostly got the night shift during the week that Ting was supposed to be wearing the cone. I had always thought cats were nocturnal but, as Ting aptly demonstrated, they're actually crepuscular, which means they're most active during twilight hours—dusk and dawn. From midnight until 5:30 a.m. or so, Ting would doze at my feet while I read book proposals or answered e-mail. But as soon as the sky started to lighten, all bets were off. She'd prowl around the house with me right behind her, then have her breakfast, then hop on the couch to groom herself—which is when I had to be hyper-vigilant, lest she try to clean her belly. Most mornings, I ended up sitting her on my lap and draping my arm across her stomach while she cleaned her face and head as the sun rose over the pond. Mom would come down around 6:00 to relieve me.

Other than routine checkups, our trips to the vet in subsequent years were for minor things: an eye infection that cleared up when we sprinkled a little L-Lysine onto her food; a bout of feline acne on her chin that went away in a week with the help of a few Oxy pads—which, make no mistake, she did not care for. On the whole she was a very healthy cat, and we saw to it that she led a happy life.

But as kittenhood transitioned into cathood and Ting became the cat with the pistachio eyes, Dad's health started to decline. His heart couldn't compensate for the bypass grafts that hadn't taken—couldn't build enough new pathways to deliver the blood and oxygen he needed. He had a stent put in, and it helped—for a time. Mom retired to be home with him.

It was me, not Mom, who'd been home alone with Dad the first time he'd had an angina attack. We were living in Cleveland then, and I must have been nine or ten. It was a crisp fall Saturday, and we were doing what we normally did at that time of year—sitting on the floor of the family room, watching the Michigan game while snacking on Little Caesars breadsticks and dipping sauce, and playing with *Star Wars* figures.

"Who's this green one?" Dad asked.

"Greedo," I said.

"Who's this fat one on the throne?"

"Jabba. He's atrocious."

It went on like that until late in the fourth quarter when the game got good, at which time I knew better than to try to engage my father in anything remotely resembling conversation.

The Wolverines were down by three and trying to get within field-goal range when my father dragged himself onto the couch. The rest of what happened comes to me in snatches—fragments due to the passage of time, or the fear I felt, or the episodic nature of childhood memory. What I recall is that his white Hanes V-neck was soaked with sweat, which was also pouring off his forehead. Me running to the kitchen to get him paper towel. Him telling me to dial Mom at work, then telling me to hang up on her and dial 911. Him saying I should unlock the front door and put Cinnamon in the bedroom. Him waving to me as the ambulance pulled away.

But now it would be Mom who'd be home with Dad if something bad were to happen. Mom and Ting, that is. Dad and Ting had developed a close bond, settling into a daily routine that involved a lot of napping, for both of them. So that he could see her as he fell asleep and as he woke, and because he knew how much she loved heights, he positioned Ting's kitty bed on top of the armoire directly across from their bed. Of course, she needed a way to get up there—the armoire was as tall as I was—so Mom and I helped Dad construct an elaborate "stairway to the stars" that included a scratching post atop two end tables, bookended for stability by a coffee table and a TV stand. The cleaning ladies must have thought we were nuts, but Ting was happy up there, so we were. Always an F. Scott Fitzgerald fan, Dad started referring to her as "the eyes of Dr. T. J. Eckleburg."

According to a ten-year study conducted by the Stroke Center at the University of Minnesota Medical Center, cats improve the health of cardiac patients. Of the more than four thousand participants in the study, those with cats showed a 30 percent lower risk of death from heart attack than those without. So said the senior author of the study, who, it should be noted, had a cat named Ninja. Mom and I had no doubt that Ting provided health benefits to Dad—that petting her, or perhaps her mere presence, lowered his stress level, and probably his heart rate and blood pressure as well. We liked to think that the families of the other 82 million pet cats in the United States were benefiting similarly.

In addition to having a calming effect on Dad, Ting was his main source of fun. Mom and Dad's bedroom floor was strewn with cat toys—a catnip-filled lobster Dad dubbed "Larry," a little felt ball with a tiny bell inside, various and sundry cotton-covered mice, a ladybug that squeaked when you poked it. We frequently entered the room to find him lying on the floor by the bed (no easy task for him to get down there), running his hand beneath the dust ruffle to locate Ting's newest favorite. Every friend or relative who called to see how he was doing got a ten-minute recap of Ting's latest antics. So did the tax guy, the handyman, the snowplow guy, and the guy who does our lawn. Anytime we couldn't find her, all we had to do was go to wherever Dad was watching TV, ask if he'd seen Ting, and her little head would pop out from beneath the collar of his robe at the sound of her name. If left undisturbed, she'd sleep against his chest like that for hours.

All of us adored Ting, but there was no question whose cat she was.

Chapter Three

Dusk

*Dawn follows Dawn, and Nights
grow old
and all the while this
curious cat . . .*

—OSCAR WILDE

Though he didn't have a cat growing up, my father had always had a soft spot for them. So when I woke up from an after-school nap one early-fall Tuesday when I was eleven or twelve, I wasn't entirely surprised to find him standing by our front window, watching a cat explore the pachysandra that encircled the giant pin oak in our front yard.

"She's healthy," he said, "not hungry. Hunting for sport, not food."

"How can you tell?" I asked him.

"It's in the way she moves."

I stood there with him for a time, observing. He was right; her moves lacked urgency. She was beautiful, though—not exotic like our cat, sturdy to Cinnamon's sleek, but a gorgeous striped tabby with a long, proud tail.

"Do you think she lives around here?"

"I do," said Dad, "but she may not be a house cat. She might be from the farms."

The next town over, Avon Lake, was rural, while ours, Bay Village, was suburban. Avon was where we got our eggs and our corn, our pumpkins and our berries. It was two blocks away from Nantucket Row, the street on which we lived—not far for a cat to wander, if a cat was so inclined.

Soon the tabby started to make her way along the row of yew shrubs that led to our front door. Dad went and opened it—just the main wooden part—and we stood and watched through the storm door, hoping the cat would come close enough for us to get a good look at her. A minute later, that's exactly what she did.

There was nothing timid about her. She sauntered onto our front porch and came right up to the door, fogging the glass with her little cat breath. She was two feet away from where we were standing, but we stayed very still and she couldn't see us. We had a good view of her, though. Her eyes were kiwi green, and they were impossibly, inexplicably lined, top and bottom, with a color best described as crème brûlée. She had no collar, but she didn't look wild. Her fur wasn't matted; she didn't have scratches, or nicked ears, or sores. Like Dad had said from the get-go, healthy.

"Should we let her in?"

Dad paused a long time before answering. "I don't think we should," he said. "She might belong to someone."

"Who would let her roam like this?" I started rattling off all the things that could harm her—cars, dogs, the neighbor boys with the BB guns.

"People raise cats different ways," he said. "Not everyone has a fenced-in yard."

"How could they not?" I asked him, puzzled.

"Some people can't afford it," he said. "Others don't like to be contained."

Neither reason made sense to me—or sense enough, at least. If you had a cat and you let it out, you should have a fence.

"But what if she's hungry? And what if she doesn't have somewhere to sleep? It gets cold at night now."

He could see he wasn't going to win this one, and truth be told, I'm not sure he wanted to.

"We'll feed her and fix her a bed," he said. "But we can't let her in the house. She has to be free to go home if she wants, and if she has fleas and we let her in, Cinnamon could get them. You don't want that, do you?"

He had me there.

The stranger cat was still at the door, so we backed away slowly and headed for the kitchen. Dad grabbed a pouch of Cinnamon's Tender Vittles and an appetizer-size paper plate to put them on. I got a plastic cup and filled it with water. We carried them to the front door and, to our delight, the cat was still there.

"You go," said Dad. "You're less intimidating."

She backed away when I opened the door, but only far enough to let me slip out. I put the water in the corner by the mailbox. Dad reached out and handed me the food, which I put down beside it. The cat watched me carefully the whole time—curious, not scared. She didn't approach me, so I didn't approach her, even though I wanted to pet her. I stepped back inside and closed the storm door. She went to the food and started eating, but not in a ravenous way. A treat had been offered and so she ate it, but this cat wasn't starving.

Dad went and found a cardboard box and a couple of bath towels Mom wouldn't miss. He pushed the flaps down into it, turned it on its side, and bunched up the towels to make a nice bed—one that the box's true bottom would shelter from the wind. The cat was done eating by then and was busy grooming herself, so Dad slipped out and placed the box in the corner closest to the house, the open part facing the wall with just enough room for the cat to squeeze in.

From back inside he and I watched her as she sniffed the box and, after a few minutes, made her way into it and settled down for the night. It was almost dark by then.

Dad and I fed the cat like this for the next three weeks and, as far as we know, she slept on our porch each night. It was late October by then, and we knew that soon it would be too cold for her. Mom took her picture and made up a flier announcing that she had been "found." I went with her to post it in the supermarket, the bowling alley, and the bank, the three highest-trafficked places in the town. She called all the local vets to see if anyone had reported a missing tabby. No one had, but she brought them flyers, too. We took out an ad in *WestLife*, our local paper. A week went by. No calls.

I started studying the weather reports in the Cleveland *Plain Dealer* religiously, and when I read that the temperature was going to dip into the 30s, I informed my parents—in that special ultimatum way that preteens always do—that if they didn't let the cat come into the house, I was going to sleep on the porch beside her to keep her warm. I also informed them that her name was Dusk, because that's what time it was when we found her, and that's what time she always came back. I figured she'd be harder to leave in the cold if she was a cat with a name.

I needn't have worried, though. Unbeknownst to me and Mom, Dad had already prepared a room for the cat—my old playroom, where Cinnamon never went. It was located at the top of the staircase that started right beside the front door. We could smuggle her up without Cinnamon seeing—without Cinnamon feeling threatened or betrayed. Dad had already put a litter box up there, and a cardboard box/bed like the one on the porch, so she'd understand that she slept here now. Dad said that his only concern was whether she'd let us pick her up and bring her in. None of us had even touched her.

Except, of course, all three of us had—when the other two weren't looking. My father confessed to it first. He'd been petting her for weeks, ever since she had started brushing up against his legs when he went to change her water. I made my confession next: She really liked behind-the-ear scratches.

"Also her chin and neck," said Mom, outing herself in the process. "But I always washed my hands right after—in the bathroom sink with soap."

It was decided that Dad would do the honors. I would man the front door and Mom would man the door to the playroom while he scooped her up and carried her upstairs. Whatever fiasco each of us was envisioning didn't come to pass. Dusk arrived around 6:30, and with it, Dusk the cat.

By 7:00 she was catching sparrows in her sleep beneath our Ping-Pong table.

We knew we could love her, but we knew we couldn't keep her—couldn't give her the run of the house because of Cinnamon, couldn't keep her upstairs like Emily Dickinson. It wouldn't be fair to her. She deserved a home of her own, with a fenced-in yard where she'd be happy and safe.

Mom started talking her up at work and, within a week, had found her a family. Dad arranged not to be there when the people came to get her. The first time I kissed her was when I kissed her good-bye.

CHAPTER FOUR

Happy Holidays

A kitten is the delight of a household. All day long a comedy is played out by an incomparable actor.

—CHAMPFLEURY

Mom is Catholic and Dad is Jewish, so in our house we celebrate both Christmas and Hanukkah. My whole childhood, both of my parents went out of their way to make sure I was exposed to both religions—and, because they loved and supported each other, it was usually Mom signing me up for JCC summer camp and Dad driving me to CCD classes.

Although it lasts for eight nights, Hanukkah is always simple: We light the menorah (Dad strikes the match; I hold the candle; Mom takes it from me and places it), exchange small gifts, and eat something vaguely Jewish, such as brisket or stuffed cabbage that Mom and I have made using a recipe we got from Aunt Harriet, Dad's sister. No special music, no silly outfits, no decorations. Easy peasy, in and out. Nice, but nondisruptive.

And then there's Christmas.

The best word to describe Christmas in the Warren house is "overkill." We actually don't go crazy on presents—maybe four or five gifts each—but we're over the top on everything else.

It begins with cookie madness. We bake raisin-topped molasses thumbprints, seven-layer bars with extra coconut, peanut butter blossoms with Hershey's kisses, gingerbread men with homemade frosting, and, of course, sugar cookies in the shape of candy canes, bells, reindeer, Santas, snowmen, trumpeting angels, stars, ornaments, and Christmas trees—all of which we top with red, white, and green sprinkles or (for the bells, stars, and angels) those little edible silver-colored balls that kind of hurt your teeth.

Next comes Dad's favorite, the icebox cake, which consists of two rows of dark brown Famous Chocolate Wafer cookies, each cookie cemented to the next with a thick layer of fresh whipped cream, to which we've added vanilla.

We secure the two rows to each other with a generous coating of more whipped cream. We chill it overnight, then cut it on the diagonal. Voilà—zebra cake.

Then it's on to the rum cake, with an emphasis on the rum. We make at least a dozen each year, keeping a couple for ourselves and gifting the rest to neighbors, colleagues, and unsuspecting friends. In theory, the rum—the main component of the icing that's drizzled across the top—burns off while we mix it in the saucepan, but we use so much (double what the recipe requires) that the cakes can pack a punch. Plus, we poke holes in the cake and pour the icing into them, upping the taste as well as the alcohol content.

To our credit, we've resisted the urge to dress Ting up in festive outfits (though a fuzzy pair of reindeer antlers once spoke to us quite loudly). This does not mean, however, that she's not a part of Christmas in other ways. In fact, Ting does her very best to ruin Christmas every year. Dad says it's because she's Jewish, and he sticks to his guns even when I remind him that Judaism is matrilineal.

Our first Christmas with Ting, we made the mistake of decorating the boxes with curling ribbon. Apparently it too-closely resembled the pigtail pipe cleaners she plays with. She shredded them—all of them—before we could stop her, tearing much of the wrapping paper in the process.

A few of the presents were in gift bags, but even they weren't spared. It turns out that Ting also liked tissue paper.

More accurately, Ting liked *licking* tissue paper. Unfortunately, we didn't notice this until Christmas morning, when we doled out spitball-covered gifts.

Mom always decorated the mantel in the living room with little china figurines of Christmas mice that we'd bought for her at the Hallmark store over the years. Her collection boasted about two dozen of them, including mouse nibbling giant peppermint, mother and father mice decorating tree, mouse on ice skates, mouse balancing on snowflake, tobogganing mice, Santa Mouse and, the coup de grâce, mouse in a manger. And all of them got displayed beneath an original Lapayese del Rio oil-on-canvas abstract still life that Mom and Dad had gotten in Madrid on their honeymoon. It was a crazy juxtaposition of kitsch and high art, which was kind of why we loved it.

When Mom arranged the mice on the mantel, we always tried to make a thing of it. Votive candles were lit. Bows made of red and green plaid were tied to every stationary object, especially our myriad animal statues—from the ceramic zebra by the TV, to the ceramic giraffe beside the old butter churn, to the metal rhinoceros on top of the antique smoking cabinet. Christmas music—namely, the "album" my high school choir put out, complete with the usual suspects, "O Holy Night" and "The Little Drummer Boy"—was played, and rum and Cokes were consumed (assuming there was any rum left after making the cakes).

When Mom was done decorating the mantel that first Christmas with Ting, I made the mistake of holding her up to have a look. At the time she showed little interest—so little, in fact, that Mom was offended. But apparently Ting was just playing it cool. Later that night, for whatever reason, Ting decided she wanted to check it out in earnest. It wasn't easy. To get to the mantel, she had to jump from the floor to the armchair to the ledge of the bay window to the TV, and then a good three feet to the mantel. And the mantel itself was very narrow. Unfortunately, Ting was very nimble.

In Ting's defense, I don't think she recognized the figurines as being mice, per se. She did, however, recognize them as being loads of fun to bat off the mantel one by one. We heard the crashing from upstairs, but in our rum-soaked state attributed the sound to icicles falling off the roof. "Oh, that's lovely," Mom had said. "Tinkle, tinkle, tinkle."

It was the next morning before we saw the mass grave of mice strewn across our living-room floor.

But Ting's biggest contribution to Christmas was the Christmas tree itself. Anticipating her inability to resist low-hanging ornaments, we had left the bottom branches unadorned except for a strand of little white lights. So as not to attract her attention, we had even declined to use the kind that blink. On the higher branches we had hung

ornaments, but only ones made of wood, fabric, paper, or metal—basically anything that couldn't or likely wouldn't break. In other words, we cat-proofed Christmas—or so we thought. What we failed to calculate, however, was Ting's agility and determination. Throughout the month of December, she had made several attempts to climb the tree, sending numerous angels cascading to the floor. Each time we heard the commotion, one of us ran over to rescue her—by which I mean pry her from the trunk claw by claw while she glared at us over her shoulder.

And then, on Christmas Eve, a miracle occurred: Ting-Pei Warren, the Judeo-Christian Buddhist cat, high on catnip and tuna water, silently scaled the six-foot spruce while her family sat by the fire, making short work of a pecan-encrusted cheese log. The three of us turned just in time to see her, a silver star atop the highest bough. And just in time to see her lose her balance and take the entire tree down with her.

Merry Christmas to all, and to all a good night.

CHAPTER FIVE

Any Given Day

I love cats because I enjoy my home; and little by little, they become its visible soul.

—JEAN COCTEAU

While holidays with Ting were never uneventful, as she grew older she mellowed considerably. Daily life with her became wonderfully routine. There's something about having a cat to take care of that regulates a family. Ting's basic needs and predictable habits, coupled with her expectations for slow movements and soft tones, superseded any desire we might otherwise have had for excitement—and that was fine with us. She had a calming effect on the house. Like all good cats, she radiated peace.

Mornings with her were Mom and Dad's favorite. As soon as one of them started to stir, Ting would use the little brown-suede stand at the base of their bed to hop up onto it and creep along their bodies until they were face-to-face. She'd nestle there between them, purring softly, until they were both awake enough to fuss over her—to drag their nails along her jaw or push her onto her side and rub her chest. Sometimes she'd start kneading, sometimes she'd doze off. Mostly, though, she just stayed for a bit, got what she needed, and then popped down. She could do so soundlessly, if she chose, or with a thud for the front paws and a thud for the hind—quick as a horse's canter.

Changing her water was Dad's job. Each morning, he'd pick up her glass from its spot in the bathroom and take it downstairs to the kitchen sink, rinse it out, and refill it—not with tap water, though; we used bottled for Ting, just like we did for ourselves, to guard against the lead we felt sure was present given the age of our house's pipes. Every couple of days, the glass would go into the dishwasher and Ting would get a clean one.

While Dad poured Ting's water, Mom took care of her food. She'd throw out whatever was left from the night before (which, generally speaking, wasn't much), wipe the dish out carefully with a Kleenex, and put down fresh.

We'd watch the dish throughout the day and replenish it as necessary, never wanting to put down too much at once, lest it get stale.

The water and the food resided beneath a print of Mondrian's *Blue Chrysanthemum*—a poster from the Guggenheim's centennial exhibition, October 8–December 12, 1971. Mom and Dad were living in Pearl River, New York, then, but they'd driven into the city for its opening, met their friends Elliot and Sharon for dinner, and then driven home. I was born nine months later, seven months to the day after the exhibit ended. The poster is special to my parents because of the timing, but I love it for the symmetry: blue cat with silver tipping, blue chrysanthemum with silver frame. I sometimes think that if the house were on fire, one of us would grab Ting, one would grab Cinnamon's ashes (which I keep on the mantel in my bedroom), and one would grab the Mondrian.

After eating her breakfast, Ting would always look to settle in the sun. In the living room, we have a print of Degas's *Ballet School*, in which a scuffed diagonal intersects a slant of light coming from a window half obscured by a spiral staircase. Lack of tulle aside, Ting would have fit right into the painting given her love of basking on hardwood floors, which she did every morning from 7:00 to 8:00 a.m., one paw stretched out in front of her as if to keep the light in place, her body absorbing the heat. When the light

PIET MONDRIAN

CENTENNIAL EXHIBITION

OCTOBER 8-DECEMBER 12, 1971   THE GUGGENHEIM MUSEUM

finally shifted, one of us would scoop her up and hold her. It was like pressing the sun against your chest.

The rest of Ting's morning was generally spent on the window ledge in the lower-level sunroom, which gets the rays for a few more hours. We'd placed a Mexican blanket there for her—a beige, royal blue, and bright yellow one that we got in Cancun back when I was in high school. It took so many washes to make it soft that all the colors have run together. In the spring Ting napped on it against a backdrop of hot pink azalea blossoms; in the winter, she blended in with the bare, gray branches. On weekdays, Mom and Dad would take turns going downstairs to check on Ting every hour or so. There was no need to, really— she was always fine—but seeing her reassured them; not just that *she* was well, but that everything was.

On weekends, I would often bring work down to the lower level and camp out on the couch beneath Ting's ledge. Writing is easier with a cat beside you. Add a blanket and a cup of tea, and I'm good for an hour—two if Mom comes down with a second cup of tea.

When Ting would hear Mom and Dad preparing lunch, she'd generally head upstairs to the kitchen and situate herself on the back of the living-room couch so she could watch them eat from afar. If lunch was tuna fish or sardines, she'd camp out on the table itself. She would never try to steal a bite; she didn't have to, as one was always offered.

After lunch came bath time—hers, not theirs. That task could be accomplished in any number of places: the big bay window in the living room, the bedroom rocking chair, a cardboard box lined with a beach towel and placed on the shelf of the closet in Mom and Dad's bedroom. Ting's only rule was that her bath could not be disturbed, because any part of her touched while bathing would have to be washed again. Once she was clean, a nap ensued. The nap would often travel—armchair to bed, carpet to couch—but regardless of where it migrated, it would usually last until dinner.

Dinnertime called for a prowl, which always made me think of my prison-guard grandfather—my mother's father—patrolling the yard. Ting would roam silently from room to room, sniffing the night air as she went, rubbing her face along the hearth, and checking out anything new—be it a brown paper bag full of cornhusks or a relocated ficus. By dessert she had settled down and would demand that attention be paid—scratching, brushing, petting, or all of the above. Then she would curl up on the couch while we read or watched TV.

Bedtime had its own rituals, of course. After the news— Mom wanted to hear the weather; Dad, the scores; and I wanted to hear some hard news that one of my authors could speak to so I could pitch them to the media the next day—one, two, or sometimes all three of us would tuck

Ting into bed, wherever she'd decided bed would be that night (a pile of laundry left in the orange armchair in my parents' room; Dad's robe bunched up in the rocking chair on Mom's side of the bed). And almost immediately she'd fall asleep, completely unaware she had anchored our day. The clocks in our house were superfluous; we marked our time by the cat.

The French novelist Colette once said, "There are no ordinary cats." And while clearly we think Ting is one of a kind, you'd be hard-pressed to find a cat we don't like. That's why it baffles me that, somehow, cats have gotten a bad rap. We all know that black ones have been pegged as harbingers of bad luck—best avoided, like walking under ladders. But a more insidious smear campaign seems to be under way, painting cats as selfish and aloof. It's foolish, really. Cats don't snub; insecure people just think they do. And I'm embarrassed to say that authors are helping to perpetuate this myth.

Some of the digs are fairly gentle, as in L. M. Montgomery's novel *Anne of the Island*: "I love them, they are so nice and selfish. Dogs are *too* good and unselfish. They make me feel uncomfortable. But cats are gloriously human."

And in Christopher Hitchens's *The Portable Atheist*: "Owners of dogs will have noticed that, if you provide them with food and water and shelter and affection, they will think you are god. Whereas owners of cats are compelled to realize that, if you provide them with food and water and shelter and affection, they draw the conclusion that *they* are gods."

Or in Gillian Flynn's *Gone Girl*: "Sleep is like a cat: It only comes to you if you ignore it." Then there's Seanan McGuire's *Rosemary and Rue*, where it says, "Cats never listen. They're dependable that way; when Rome burned, the emperor's cats still expected to be fed on time."

Even poets have participated:

Before a Cat will condescend
To treat you as a trusted friend,
Some little token of esteem
Is needed, like a dish of cream.
—T. S. Eliot, "The Ad-dressing of Cats,"
Old Possum's Book of Practical Cats

The cat criticism is often more barbed, though. James Thurber once said: "I am not a cat man, but a dog man, and all felines can tell this at a glance—a sharp, vindictive glance." In Jodi Picoult's novel, *House Rules,* a character says, "I think cats have Asperger's." And the fur really flies in Jonathan Franzen's novel, *Freedom*: "Walter had never liked cats. They'd seemed to him the sociopaths of the pet world."

Thankfully, though, there are some authors who "get" cats and who vouch for them. Take, for example, Robertson Davies, who said, "Authors like cats because they are such quiet, lovable, wise creatures, and cats like authors for the same reasons." And Ernest Hemingway, who pronounced: "A cat has absolute emotional honesty: human beings, for one reason or another, may hide their feelings, but a cat does not." And Mark Twain, who attested, "If animals could speak, the dog would be a blundering outspoken fellow; but the cat would have the rare grace of never saying a word too much." And Anne Morrow Lindbergh, who supplied, "I saw the most beautiful cat today. It was sitting by the side of the road, its two front feet neatly and graciously together. Then it gravely swished around its tail to completely encircle itself. It was so fit and beautifully neat, that gesture, and so self-satisfied."

But perhaps Charles Dickens said it best: "What greater gift than the love of a cat."

The author Andre Dubus, whose books I publicized in the '90s when I worked at David R. Godine, a small literary press in Boston, once told me that he thought short-story writers had more in common with poets than they did with novelists. I think he was right. But I've always seen an even stronger connection between poets and painters—always thought they were cut from the same cloth. Both create something that's painstakingly exact yet open to interpretation.

No two people will see the same thing when they look at a Vermeer, or a Seurat, or a Rembrandt, or a Cezanne, just like no two people will have the same reaction to a poem by E. E. Cummings or Anna Akhmatova, or Elizabeth Bishop or Wallace Stevens. And, of course, the Imagist movement in poetry, which strove to express so much through so little—concise language and precise images—is in its restraint redolent of the Impressionist movement in art, with its truncated brushstrokes, and the Pointillism movement, with its dabs of paint.

In graduate school, while studying to get my MFA in poetry, I became further intrigued by the connections between poets and painters, whether friendships like that between Gertrude Stein and Pablo Picasso, or instances where a poet found inspiration in a painting, or a painter in a poem. My final project—a book-length collection of poems—contained verse inspired by Edward Hopper's *Rooms by the Sea*, Chinese artist Chao Shao-an's *Early Snow on Lotus Pond*, and Amedeo Modigliani's *Portrait of Jeanne Hébuterne*, to name a few. For my final paper, I attempted to translate some of Picasso's poems into English. You'd think a Cubist would have had better line breaks.

But Picasso redeemed himself in my eyes when I saw his cat paintings—and there are more of them than I would have thought, including the admittedly disturbing *Wounded Bird and Cat* (for a gentler pairing, see Paul Klee's *Cat and Bird*) and the slightly perplexing *Lying Female Nude with Cat* (it looks to be a kitten, not a cat, and it presents a couple of anatomical quandaries). But for reasons that are probably self-explanatory, I'm most drawn to his *Crazy Woman with Cats*.

The number of influential artists who've painted cats is astounding. Henri Rousseau's *The Tiger Cat* has a Picasso-esque quality to it—the angular, almost pieced-together face—as does Fernand Léger's *Woman with a Cat*, with its puzzle-piece person and puzzle-piece cat. Mary Cassatt's *Children Playing with a Cat* is a puzzle, too—but not literally this time. It's perplexing because the cat's not playing at all; it's completely conked out in the little girl's lap.

Cassatt's fellow Impressionist, Pierre-Auguste Renoir, was also intrigued by children and cats, giving us *Young Boy with a Cat* and *L'Enfant au Chat (Mademoiselle Julie Manet)*, where the child looks pensive but the cat is the epitome of contentment. That child was, in fact, the niece of painter Édouard Manet, who himself contributed *Madame Manet with a Cat* (I think, if you're a painter, at some point you have to paint your wife with her cat—that is, if you want her to stay your wife) and *Les Chats* (three small cat etchings on a single sheet of paper; I'm not a tattoo type, but if I were, they'd be contenders).

But back to Renoir, who also painted *La Jeune Fille au Chat* ("Young Girl with a Cat") and *Sleeping Girl* (aka, "Girl with a Cat"). It's worth noting that, in the latter painting, the cat is sleeping, too, his right paw resting in the girl's left hand. The girl looks exhausted. She's wearing sensible shoes. Her skirt is blue and her cat is blue, and from a distance you can't tell them apart. In the same vein as

Sleeping Girl, there's Renoir's *Sleeping Cat*. "Looks familiar," Mom said, nodding in Ting's direction when I showed her Renoir's ball of a cat.

But my favorite Renoir painting is *Woman with Cat*. It was done almost a hundred years before I was born, and yet it's so familiar. The woman holds her tabby the same way we hold Ting—cheek to cheek, her left arm supporting the cat's back legs. Her skin is pale, her eyebrows dark. There's no ring on her finger, but she's happy.

It'd be a challenge to find a major artist of the nineteenth or twentieth century who didn't paint—or at least sketch—a cat. There's Vincent van Gogh's *Hand with Bowl and a Cat*, done in black chalk. There's Paul Gauguin's *Mimi and Her Cat* (gouache on cardboard) and his *Little Cat*, which I like even better ("Would go great in our living room," said Mom, of the black, leopard-like cat crawling toward brown and burnt-orange balls). And speaking of black cats, there's Henri Matisse's *Girl with a Black Cat*, in which neither of them look particularly pleased.

On the other end of the color spectrum is Pierre Bonnard's *The White Cat* (oil on canvas, longest legs ever). Bonnard also painted *Sitting Woman with a Cat*, where the curve of the woman's dress melts into the curve of the cat's tail. Yes.

And of course there's German Expressionist Franz Marc, lover of vibrant colors. When he wasn't painting deer, he was painting cats—a prolific cat-chronicler if ever there was one. *Two Cats, Blue and Yellow* and *Cat on a Yellow Pillow* are my favorites. But I also like *Cats, Red and White, Three Cats, Cat Behind a Tree,* and *Girl with Cat.*

If I had a dime for every painter with a painting titled *Girl with Cat*—or something like it. The names of the paintings are downright boring. How interesting, though, that cats are almost always portrayed by painters not as the solitary animals so many authors have made them out to be, but as communal creatures who take delight in their human companions.

Cats and painters. Painters and cats. Not only are cats the frequent subject of paintings, they have also been the beloved pets of painters. And that's where things get sad. Some of the most cat-loving painters never actually painted their cats—or anyone else's, as far as I know. Chief among them, Viennese painter Gustav Klimt, who liked cats so much he permitted them in his studio, and even allowed them to play among his sketches. As Lee Hendrix, senior curator of drawings at the J. Paul Getty Museum, said, "[Klimt] posed models on a bed so that their languorous bodies could suggest floating, a motif that's very important in his art." It seems he had another reason for posing his models on a bed. Klimt fathered at least fourteen children, mostly with said models. If only he hadn't been so busy "studying" the human form—and, sadly, contracting syphilis. His love of lines would have lent itself so beautifully to the feline form.

There are three other painters who may or may not have had cats, but who, to my great disappointment, didn't paint them. The first is French Impressionist Edgar Degas, who chose the ballerina as his muse when the lithe, supple cat was there for the offering. He should have taken his cue from Leonardo da Vinci, who did a twenty-three-drawing *Study of Cat Movements and Positions*, and concluded: "The smallest feline is a masterpiece." The second is Amedeo Modigliani, who chose to paint the long, sad oval of the human face instead of the fine and angular face of the feline. And the third is Edward Hopper. All those windows, and not a cat in them. All that light to bask in, wasted.

CHAPTER SIX

Good Fences

A dog is a dog, a bird is a bird, and a cat is a person.
—MUGSY PEABODY

Our house on Stillwater Pond is located on an old apple orchard that was once part of the Searles estate. Edward Francis Searles was born on July 4, 1841, and died in 1920 at the age of seventy-nine. In between, the interior and architectural designer married one of his richest clients, Mary Frances Hopkins. Twenty-two years his senior, she was the widow of railroad tycoon Mark Hopkins, one of the four founders of the Central Pacific Railroad. Searles met her while designing her home in Great Barrington,

Massachusetts—a three-year project that ended in 1888, one year after they married. When she died in 1891, he inherited $21 million and the house he'd built for her, along with real estate in San Francisco and New York. He also inherited property in Methuen, Massachusetts, the town on the other side of our pond.

Searles spent the rest of his life engaged in what one historian has called "obsessive castle building," often in collaboration with the well-known Boston architect Henry Vaughan. One of their projects was the least ornate of Searles's six houses, the main house at Stillwater Manor, which is visible from the front window of my parents' room—the one where Ting suns herself in the late afternoons. The Manor House, as it's known around here, is a three-story, twenty-four-room mansion built in 1905 in a Tudor/Elizabethan style, with its vertical and diagonal timber frame and whitewashed wattle-and-daub walls. Elsewhere on the property is the Carriage House. All of it is surrounded by castle walls, with a gate we drive through daily to get to our much simpler home.

In addition to being a lover of grand structures, Edward Searles was something of an environmentalist. He wouldn't hesitate to change the course of a stone wall if a tree was in the way. A swinger of birches, Robert Frost would have liked him—and may have. In Derry, New Hampshire—a mere dozen miles from the Manor House in Salem—is the

Robert Frost Farm, where the poet lived with his family from 1900 to 1911, and which served as fodder for many of his greatest poems, including "Mending Wall." The two men were contemporaries, and practically neighbors. In fact, the Frost Farm was just six miles up the road from Searles Castle, Searles's more elaborate home in Windham, made of sandstone from his own quarries.

Nature and respect for it are tenets of Stillwater Circle; always have been, from what I can tell. It's one of the things that drew us here, because it's one of our basic tenets, too. But as anyone who lives in New Hampshire will tell you, nature can be a pain in the ass. Don't take my word for it, however; take Ting-Pei's.

It was a sunny Monday in spring when Ting-Pei alerted Mom and Dad to a commotion in the fireplace. Thinking that a bird must have come down the chimney, Mom told Dad to open the window while she went and got an old bedsheet. Back downstairs, she held one end of the sheet up to the fireplace and Dad held the other. He reached down and unlatched the glass doors.

"Ready?" he asked her.

"Ready," she said. And with that, he flung them open.

They were expecting the bird to fly into the sheet so they could trap it and carry it to the window, where they figured it would know what to do. The bird, however, had other ideas. From behind the sheet came a hissing noise, a cloud of ash, and a whole lot of thwacking. Mom was so startled that she dropped her corner, screaming, "That's no bird!"

Technically she was wrong. It wasn't a warbler, or a blue jay, or a thrush, a tufted titmouse, or a yellow-shafted flicker. It wasn't a catbird or a mockingbird, which we used to confuse until Dad pointed out that the catbird was gray, like Ting. It wasn't any of the small, pretty birds that reside on our property and that my parents were expecting. It wasn't even a pigeon or a mourning dove or crow. It was certainly avian, but at that moment it was mainly a giant black object flying at Mom's face.

"Duck," Mom screamed, so that's what Dad did, crouching beneath the mantel.

"No, you idiot—it's a duck!"

And so it was—a female wood duck, wild-eyed and covered in soot, right down to the tips of her iridescent wings. She must have been trying to build a nest on our chimney when she fell down into it, *kerplunk.*

The story would have ended there if Dad had opened the window like Mom had asked. But he had thought better of it while she was upstairs, afraid that Ting might fall out. He had reasoned that the bird, once ensconced in the sheet, would be easy enough to take out the front door. But that was back when it was a wren or a chat, not a two-pound wood duck with a three-foot wingspan.

The terrified duck flew around the room, brushing against everything as she went. We had just had the whole place painted, of course: Benjamin Moore Mystic Beige. Now the room looked like a Pollock painting, thick black brushstrokes on every wall.

The duck finally landed on the bay window ledge. Mom snatched the sheet from Dad, threw it over the duck, cranked open the window, and pushed the duck toward it.

And where was Ting during all of this? Under the kitchen table, of course, about as helpful as my father, who rose up from his crouch just in time to see Mom scoot the duck off the ledge.

Ting was a bit more obliging when it came to the field mouse—but only a bit. Our laundry room is on the lower level, and it's strictly off limits to Miss Ting-Pei Warren. Too many nooks and crannies where she could get into trouble, most of them crammed with insulation and pipes. She is, of course, fascinated by the place, as anyone would be by something so close but so completely out of reach. She became even more fascinated with it, however, when a field mouse established residence.

February in New Hampshire is always bitter cold, but this year it was particularly brutal—well below zero with the wind chill factored in. Dad had taken to wearing a ski cap around the house, to keep his bald head warm. Mom wore silk long underwear beneath her turtleneck and polar fleece. The thermostat read 70 degrees, but our high-ceilinged rooms were considerably colder—cold enough, in fact, that in the mornings and evenings we could see our breath. To a field mouse, however, it was positively toasty compared to the great outdoors. And so one came in, through some crack or hole, and set up camp between the washer and dryer.

A wood and metal mousetrap was out of the question. Barbaric things, those. We researched glue traps, but they sounded just as awful. Luckily, in the process, we stumbled onto a website for humane mousetraps—the catch-and-release kind. We bundled up, laced our boots, and ventured forth to Walmart.

Fast-forward one week. Then fast-forward two. The traps were empty (we'd set three, labeled Donna, Jerry, and Lissa), the mouse was still living in the lap of luxury, and we were quickly running out of clean clothes. It wasn't that we were afraid to go into the laundry room with the mouse in there (we knew he'd hide at the sound of our footsteps); it's that we're softies and didn't want to disturb him. The washing machine had a tendency to thump, and to a mouse the dryer would sound like a tornado. But make no mistake, we wanted him gone. Not traumatized, but gone.

Ting wanted him gone, too—but in a different way. She wanted him gone from the laundry room and into our sunroom so that she could chase him. Afraid she'd somehow miss the mouse's grand exit, she took to guarding the laundry room 24/7. This worried Dad, especially.

"Did you feel her nose?" he asked me and Mom. "It's so cold. And her ears—my God, her ears."

"Yes," said Mom, "they're a little chilly."

"Chilly?" Dad barked. "She's almost hypothermic!"

"If she's cold she'll come upstairs," reasoned Mom.

"Neglect," muttered Dad. "Neglect."

Disgusted by what he perceived to be a terrible lack of concern on Mom's part, Dad decided to take action. He dragged a chair from the sunroom to the laundry-room door, where Sergeant Ting was stationed, picked her up, sat himself down, and stuffed her in his robe. I passed them an hour later on the way to my room. Her purring was audible; so was his snoring. His action was inaction, and it was working like a charm.

I don't know how long they stayed like that—I went to my room to read—but at some point I heard running and screaming in the sunroom next door. I went to have a look. Feeling a bit neglected herself, Mom had apparently snuck downstairs to see what Ting and Dad were up to. She decided to check on the mouse while there, and had left the door open a crack by mistake.

The mouse saw his shot at freedom and ran right past her into the hall. Ting, hearing him scurry by, shot out of Dad's arms. She chased the little brown mouse into the

sunroom, where they commenced playing Whac-A-Mole between the flowerpots. Mom grabbed an empty one and placed it over the mouse just like a cake-stand cover. Dad, suddenly a man of action, grabbed a nearby copy of *The New Yorker* and slid it under the flowerpot, thus trapping our houseguest so that he could be shown the door. Game over, Ting bolted upstairs to the bedroom.

More trouble than they were worth, those mice.

But the animal that vexed Ting the most was the one we called her "boyfriend bunny." For an entire summer, without missing a day, a little gray rabbit came by to see her, almost always at ten a.m. He would sit by the back door and wait for her, and because it was glass, he could see her coming. The second she walked in, he'd stand on his hind legs.

"He's myopic," said Dad. "He thinks she's a rabbit. She's gray and about his size."

Whatever the rabbit thought Ting was, Ting knew what the rabbit was, and objected. She would go to the door and stare at him, and he'd inch forward until they were nose to nose. The first few weeks she hissed at him, but as the summer wore on, he wore her down. She learned to tolerate his presence.

Fall arrived at last, and the bunny stopped coming. Ting searched for him for a couple of days, then put him out of her mind. Her space was her space, her sun, her sun. She didn't want to share it. *Something there is that doesn't love a wall.* Ting wasn't one of those somethings.

CHAPTER SEVEN

Party of One

A cat, however, is never without the potentialities of contentment. Like a superior man, he knows how to be alone and happy.

—H. P. LOVECRAFT

We Warrens rarely learn our lesson. After Ting had been with us for a few years, we got to thinking that, as happy as she was with her human companions, she might appreciate a playmate—a little, feline playmate. We weren't stupid enough to think that Ting would want a sibling. Ting had been raised as an only child, just like me, and we couldn't imagine her sharing her home with another cat on a daily basis. But somehow we managed to convince ourselves that she might be up for a playdate. That was mistake number one.

Mistake number two was our selection. We quickly ruled out our neighbor's cat, Lulu. Though sweet-tempered, she was a very big girl, and we were afraid she'd play too rough—without meaning to, of course. A man with whom Dad used to play bridge had a perfectly nice Persian named Buster. But Persians shed and, if they didn't get along, Ting would have reminders for days or weeks after—on the couch, on the carpet, everywhere. There was Gus, cousin Sonya's black-and-white longhair, but Nashua was forty-five minutes away, and it seemed like asking a lot of Sonya to pack her up and haul her to Salem.

We briefly flirted with the idea of taking out a personal ad, but really, what would it say? "Insanely spoiled purebred seeks same"? "SGF (single gray feline) seeks buddy for mischief and napping"? And where would we place it? The *Boston Globe*? Too expensive. The *Boston Herald*? Republican. The *Boston Phoenix*? A bit too alt. Craigslist could be creepy, and JDate wasn't around yet (never mind the fact that Ting wasn't technically Jewish and, also, that Ting was a cat).

Enter Esmé, named after the Salinger story. Like Ting, Esmé was a Korat. I thought Ting-Pei might be more at ease with a cat who looked a lot like her—that there'd be a familiarity, a certain level of comfort. They could even be related, the Korat gene pool being as small as it is. Esmé was a bruiser compared to Ting—almost eleven pounds—but I knew her to be a good, gentle cat, and, what's more, I was friends with her father. What I didn't know was whether she was a particularly *social* cat—but, then again, I didn't know if Ting was, either. After much discussion we decided to give it a try.

On a cool afternoon in April, Esmé came over to play. Her dad carried her in and set her down in the living room. Like any well-adjusted cat, she started having a look around—jumped up on the window ledge, checked out a bit of ivy. She seemed perfectly at ease here. Excited I'd found a friend for Ting—perhaps a long-lost cousin—I went upstairs to fetch her. From the second I brought Ting down the stairs, I realized we'd made a bad miscalculation. Here's a transcript of what ensued:

Esmé: Sniff. Hello. Sniff. Meow.
Ting-Pei: Crouch, growl, hiss. Whap whap.
Esmé: Sniff. Sniff. Mew?
Ting-Pei: Die! Die! Die!

By that point Ting had rolled on her back and was thumping poor Esmé with her powerful hind feet, her

canine teeth bared and glistening in the sun. Before I could make it across the room, Esmé's dad had swooped in to save her. Embarrassed, I muttered an apology as I bent to pick up Ting. I could feel her heart racing, her body tense from her encounter with the vile gray intruder with the cute and literary name—the beast from beyond that Mommy Lissa, clearly a traitor, had invited to the house.

Our guests left quickly and, within an hour, Ting had forgiven me. I'd learned an important lesson, though: Don't mess with another person's solitude—and by *person*, I mean *cat*.

CHAPTER EIGHT

Ting Is Missing

As anyone who has ever been around a cat for any length
of time well knows, cats have enormous patience with the
limitations of the human kind.

—CLEVELAND AMORY

I'm a homebody. I travel for work, but not much else. My
parents, however, especially my mom, love to take excur-
sions—the more exotic, the better. Since I graduated
from college and moved back home—meaning, since they
acquired a free, live-in cat sitter—they've gone to Ireland
(Mom's choice; her maiden name is McKittrick), Hawaii
(Dad's choice; when he was in the navy, he was stationed at

Pearl Harbor), Scotland, St. John's, Aruba, St. Martin, Cancún, Cabo San Lucas, Curaçao, Bonaire, Australia, China, and Costa Rica.

My parents brought back a present for me every time they traveled, and it was always the same thing: a cat figurine. With each one came a story—of the cats they saw while there, and the role of the cat in that country's culture.

Given my roots, I'll start with Ireland. The Irish cat figurine is jet black—heavy like a paperweight, supposedly carved from Irish turf. It was made in Ballyshannon, a town in County Donegal that looks over an estuary and claims to be Ireland's oldest. The cat is curled up and sleeping, its head resting on its right front paw, its tail curved around its haunches. Ireland has the legend of the Kilkenny cats— two cats who battled to the death and devoured each other until just their tails remained. Lovely story, that. But it's a symbol of Irish scrappiness.

My parents' trip to Scotland resulted in another black cat—a tall, thin one with perky ears and oh-so-perfect posture. Unlike in America, in Scotland (and the rest of the UK, for that matter), black cats portend good luck. Not Si-Sawat-level good luck, of course, but good luck all the same.

My parents went to China for two weeks, so they brought home *two* figurines. From Shanghai, an alabaster one with its tail tucked under its chin, and from Beijing, a basketful of cats made of ivory (synthetic, of course; we're pro-elephant here), complete with handle and lid and, near its base, two ink-drawn flowers. They shared what the shop clerk had told them: that dogs have long been the pets of hunters, and cats, the pets of farmers. For that reason, China, an agrarian nation, strongly favored the cat. Recently, eight five-thousand-year-old cat bones were found in the Chinese farming village of Quanhucun. Testing showed that one of them was from an elderly cat who probably couldn't have survived in the wild. It suggests a certain level of domestication—that the farmers must have protected the cat—and it was quite surprising to archaeologists, because cats were thought to have been domesticated a mere four thousand years ago, and in a completely different country.

One of Mom and Dad's trips to Cancún yielded a pair of tiny clay cats, one sitting up on its haunches, alert; the other, asleep in a ball. Mayan designs in black and brick-red covered their shoulders and backs. In Mexico, it's all about the jaguar, not the domestic cat; they had various jaguar gods, in fact. So it wasn't just in Egypt that cats were worshipped.

My parents always liked going to Cancún. They had a time-share there. It was quick and easy to get to, exotic but also familiar. It was black bean soup, and grilled tomatillos, and huevos rancheros for brunch.

But their favorite trip—by far, their favorite trip—was a three-week safari to Africa in 1999.

They selected Tanzania for one reason, and one reason only (though it was actually three): lion, leopard, and cheetah—the Big Cats. It took a few days of tenting on the Serengeti, but eventually, with the help of their guide, they managed to see all three in their natural habitat. They even got to see a mama lion nursing her month-old cubs.

Ting was a still-energetic four-year-old at the time, and was used to receiving all of my parents' attention. I left the office right at five each night while they were gone and went directly home to her. The first week she seemed fine, but by week two she was clearly bored and lonely, following me from room to room while I warmed up the Bagel Bites I'd been living off of for ten days, or did laundry, or looked in my father's desk for stamps, or changed out of my work clothes.

The second Thursday night that Mom and Dad were gone, Ting seemed particularly needy. It was garbage night, though, which meant I had work to do: change the litter box, empty the kitchen pail, tie up the little bag in the bathroom, then drag all of it to the giant bin in the garage so that first thing in the morning I could roll it out in front of the garage and leave it for the garbagemen.

Ting was underfoot the whole time, which was funny while I was doing her box (she christened it before I could finish pouring the litter) but annoying when I was trying to gather the trash. At one point I gave her a firm "Could you stop?" and it seemed to do the trick.

Chores done, I settled down in front of the TV in my parents' room. After an hour or so it dawned on me that Ting was being a very good girl. Too good of a girl, in fact. And where was she, anyway? She wasn't in her spot on top of Dad's armoire, or on the back of the bedroom couch, or curled up at the bottom of the bed, or asleep in her favorite rocker. Could she be under the bed pouting because I'd been a little stern with her? Entirely possible, I thought. Like the rest of the Warrens, that cat knew how to sulk.

During the next commercial I looked beneath the bed. Nope, not there. Must be on a shelf in Mom and Dad's closet (we always left the closet door open in case she felt like exploring). The commercial after that, I turned off the TV and crept over to the closet to listen for snoring. Silence. So much for the closet theory.

Still not worried—she had pulled this disappearing act before—I went back to watching TV. But when the show ended I decided I'd better walk around and find her. I started with my bedroom. Not under the desk, not under the bed, not on the floor of my closet. Family room? No. Not under the coffee table, not under the couch, not among the plants in front of the fireplace. Even though the door to the laundry room had been shut all night, I went in there to look. No dice.

Top of the fridge? No. Inside the kitchen cupboards? No, no, no, and no. She couldn't fit in a kitchen drawer, could she? Hmm, apparently not. Behind the TV in the living room? It'd be a tight squeeze, but I looked anyway. Not there.

I was starting to get pretty concerned. "Ting," I called from room to room. "Ting-Pei Warrrr-ennnn." I walked all around the house waving one of her favorite toys—a wand with a string of feathers dangling from the end of it—sure that the whirring noise would attract her, sure she'd pop right out. She didn't. I went from room to room, shaking her bag of cat food. Nope. I opened three cans of tuna, one for each level of the house, certain that would entice her. Nothing.

I started getting creative in that special way people do when someone they love is, like, ten minutes late. Could she have impaled herself on a coat hanger? I spent twenty minutes taking every item out of my parents' closet, just to make sure she hadn't—wide-lapel suit jackets from the '70s, paisley-print dresses with shoulder pads from the '80s, canvas purses, leather shoes, leather purses, canvas shoes, various and sundry baseball caps—piling all of them on the bed until the bedspread disappeared. Could she have somehow opened the toilet lid, fallen in and, in an effort to climb out, shut the lid on herself and suffocated? I checked all three of our toilets. Could she have shimmied up the chimney in a crazy reverse Santa? Hard to do because the flue was closed, but I took a flashlight and looked.

I checked the oven, the refrigerator, the freezer, the dishwasher, the washing machine, and the dryer. I went back and looked in the microwave. I peeked in the bread machine. No. Cat. Anywhere. Panic was setting in.

And then the phone rang. First thought: Somehow Ting-Pei has gotten out through the skylight and the neighbors can see her on the roof. Second thought: Cat burglar burglared my cat and is calling to ask for ransom. Third thought: Does Ting-Pei know how to dial?

But it was just my parents, calling from Africa on a solar-powered phone that cost them ten dollars per minute. It was the first time I'd talked to them in a week. And the first words out of Dad's mouth: "How's my Tinger?"

I did what any good daughter would have done in that situation—I lied through my teeth. And after Dad had me "put Ting on the phone," I assured him her ears had perked up at the sound of his voice and that she'd even licked the receiver. Dad was delighted. I was sure if Hell existed, I was destined for it.

The call was mercifully short—they had giraffes to see and were fearful of solar flares and, besides, it was expensive. I resumed my Ting hunt the second they hung up. Even though there was no way she could have gotten out of the house, I took the flashlight, slid out the front door,

and started to patrol the perimeter. Rhododendron, azalea, broken drainpipe, arborvitaes, garden hose, pissed-off possum. I made a full circle. No sign of Ting. As a general rule, Korats don't come when they're called—they're not that kind of cat—but I hollered her name a few more times while standing on the front stoop, then hurried back inside, terrified that, by this time next week, we'd be dredging the pond for her little gray body.

And then it hit me: heights, she liked heights. Maybe she was in a basket on top of the cupboards, or behind some books on the bookshelf. Flashlight still in hand, I ran to the garage where we kept a six-foot stepladder. Of course it was all wedged in. Cut to me standing barefoot on the hood of my car, trying to get some leverage, flashlight stuffed down the front of my pants. The ladder didn't budge, so I hopped down and, in the process, knocked over a rake. I bent to pick it up and, out of the corner of my eye, I thought I saw something move. I took a deep breath and prayed that, whatever it was, it wouldn't try to eat me. I crouched down and shined the light beneath my car.

And there, in all her glory, was Miss Ting-Pei Warren, covered in cobwebs, dead leaves, and something that looked like paint but wasn't. Her expression said *Took ya long enough.* Trying to look nonchalant, I walked back in the house. A moment later, Ting scurried in behind me. Religious bathing of the cat ensued, using multiple lukewarm washcloths.

I never told my parents about Ting-Pei's big adventure, and I only felt a little guilty about it. We have a long family history of telling pet-related lies. Chief among them, the death of our cairn terrier, Oregano, when I was six and a half.

I was a terrible sleeper as a child—not your garden variety "There are monsters under my bed," but more of a "Will you sit with me until I fall asleep?," followed by three hours of sitting, during which time I would pepper whichever unfortunate parent had drawn Lissa duty that night with questions like "Are bird bones hollow?" "What does 'gay' mean?" and "If I pray for a baby of my own, will I get one?"

So when Oregano passed away in her sleep at the ripe old age of fifteen, my parents agreed that telling me the truth would lead me to the natural conclusion that I, too, was unlikely to make it to morning, and that the three hours of sitting would turn into four or five. Hence, they concocted a somewhat elaborate story: that Oregano had been at the vet, very sick, for the past couple of days, and that, sadly, she had died there that morning. In truth, she had died in her doggie bed in the alcove by the kitchen.

I cried over Oregano for weeks—she was a very sweet dog, and I loved her—but my parents' plan worked, in that at least I didn't think *I'd* die in my sleep. Unfortunately, they had failed to factor in the guilt I would feel over not having noticed that Oregano had been missing from the house for days (which, of course, she hadn't), and the guilt I would feel over having focused my attention on our new cat, Cinnamon, who I was busy dressing in a baby bonnet and pushing around in a pram.

It would be a decade before I'd learn the truth about Oregano—by accident, from a comment my mother made in passing. As for why we named two pets after spices, that, I will never know. Mom's Irish; we don't even use salt.

And then there's the story of the freeze-dried robin.

When my parents and I moved from New York to Tennessee when I was five, they had a hard time finding a house to buy, and ended up having to store our furniture and move us into an apartment while they continued looking. I tagged along with them to most of the open houses, and in one of them we found a fledgling robin who had somehow gotten inside—quite a while ago, judging from the copious amount of poop in the otherwise-beautiful master bedroom. My parents contemplated setting the bird outside beneath a hydrangea, in the hope its mother would find it and that, until then, it would at least have shade. But it seemed unlikely she'd come back to claim it. Figuring we were the robin's best chance, we brought the bird back to our apartment and spent the next few days trying, in vain, to get it to eat the worms that Dad dug up from the little patch of lawn between the parking lot and the sidewalk.

You know how this story ends: The baby robin died. Mom proposed a funeral, but I didn't want to bury the bird on the apartment grounds. Better, I thought, to wait and bury it in our backyard—once we had a backyard—so we could visit the grave whenever we wanted. Mom, conscious of the emotional toll a move can take on a five-year-old, thought it best not to add to my stress. So she did what any reasonable woman would do: She put the robin in a Ziploc and placed it in the freezer.

In took them two months to find a house. By then, I'd completely forgotten about the bird. On moving day, while Dad and I waited in his idling two-door turquoise Vega— the last "bachelor car" he would ever have—Mom ran into the apartment to have a final look around the place, "just to make sure we didn't forget anything." On her way back to the car, she tossed the bird in the Dumpster.

My grandmother, too, was a disposer of birds. After two years of living in Memphis, Dad got a great job opportunity in Cleveland. When it came time to go there to look for a house—or at least to narrow down a suburb in which to search—my grandparents, who were staying with us that summer, volunteered to watch the cat. They didn't watch her closely enough, however, because when one of my zebra finches escaped from its cage, Cinnamon caught her and ate her. Or half of her, actually—the bottom half— which is how my grandmother identified the remains as being that of Chi Chi, the white-headed one with the spot on its chest. The female.

Concerned I'd be upset about the loss of Chi Chi and apoplectic that Cinnamon had committed the crime, Grampa used the Polaroid we'd given him for his birthday to take a picture of the corpse, and he and Nonnie, by then in their seventies, drove to six different pet stores in the Memphis area (with which they weren't the least bit familiar) in 100-degree heat to try to find a finch that they could pass off as Chi Chi. None of the birds were an exact match, but they did find one that came pretty close, brought it home, and proceeded with the swap-out.

I'm embarrassed to say I never noticed the difference. Apparently neither did Chester, Chi Chi's mate, who a month later became the father of three adorable babies—Chico, Chirpie, and Checkers (even at a young age, I was into alliteration). They looked a lot like their mother—by which I mean Chi Chi *dos*.

Nonnie had practice pulling bird-related fast ones. Take the case of Huey, Dewey, and Louie, the ducks she and Grampa gave my mom for Easter when she was four years old. They lived happily in a pen in my grandparents' backyard until one escaped and the neighbor dog got it. Hearing the commotion, Nonnie ran outside and, seeing the half-dead duck, wrapped it in her apron, brought it into the kitchen, and tried to revive it by pouring whiskey down its throat—which worked about as well as you'd think, and which confused poor Mom, who couldn't figure out why Nonnie had only invited one duck in for "tea."

Fearful for the remaining ducks, and not wanting to have to tell my mom that little Louie hadn't made it, Nonnie and Grampa made the difficult decision to send "all three ducks" to Grampa's father's farm, ten miles away. They sat Mom down and explained to her that the ducks were getting big and needed room to play, and that her Grampa McKittrick's farm had a giant pond where they'd be very happy. They assured her that she'd see them every time she went to visit. Mom wasn't quite buying it, though. She asked what the ducks could play on the pond that they couldn't play in the yard. Nonnie's answer: hopscotch.

Now Grampa McKittrick had been a farmer his entire life. He saw ducks as dinner, not pets—something my grandparents had somehow failed to factor into the equation. Suffice it to say, Mom never saw Huey, Dewey, or Louie playing hopscotch on the pond, and Grampa McKittrick became very good at saying "Gosh, they were there yesterday."

So we lied, all of us, about our pets. But we all had the same good reason: each other.

CHAPTER NINE

Cats and Their Companion Animals

If I'm taking a walk and I see a cat, I'm happy.
—HARUKI MURAKAMI

It's hard to know what to call Ting. The term *pet* makes her sound somehow lesser-than—lesser than us; lesser than what, or who, she is. Somehow it belittles her. It's too cutesy; it doesn't do her justice. I've heard people use the term *companion animal* to describe their dogs and cats, and while in some ways calling her that would be as silly as calling a husband a "companion human," it does at least come closer to expressing her place in our lives. It offers a certain respect. It's a nod to what every person who loves cats knows—that life would be much lonelier without them, and that while they weren't put on this planet just to keep us company, they do so with a skill and devotion that very few humans can match. That very few humans would try to.

I also like the term *companion animal* because it sounds reciprocal. As much as Ting is our companion, we are hers. She didn't choose to come here, but she wouldn't choose to leave. This is her home now, and we're her family. We're *her* companion animals.

Around the time Ting became a teenager—at least, in terms of human years—Dad's health really started to decline. In addition to his ever-present heart issues, a lingering sinus infection permanently robbed him of his ability to smell or taste—and for a man who liked to eat as much as my father liked to eat, that wasn't an insignificant thing. He said what bothered him about it most, though, was not being able to smell Ting—the warm, sweet scent of her.

Dad was also having trouble with his hearing. Growing sick of having to repeat herself and tired of having to listen to a blaring TV—and concerned about the way hearing loss can isolate a person—Mom prodded Dad to get a hearing test, and, finally, he relented. It showed measurable loss in both ears, and the audiologist suggested a hearing aid for the worst side. Dad was in his seventies by then, but still insisted he was too young for "assistive devices." He seemed so offended by the suggestion, so adamant about not needing one, that Mom and I let it ride. We learned to just speak up, and it became such a habit that we often spoke loudly to each other even when Dad wasn't in the room. When we caught ourselves doing it, all we could do was laugh.

Dad was having vision problems, too. He started missing steps on his way from the living room up to the bedroom, started having trouble seeing the squares of his crossword puzzles. Suspecting cataracts or the need for bifocals, Mom made him an appointment with the eye doctor. Tests showed something worse: a pucker on the retina of his left eye that created a blind spot in the center, similar to what someone with macular degeneration would have. Driving home from the appointment, Dad told Mom that, for the first time in his life, he felt old.

But worst of all was his back, and the tingling pain that radiated down his legs. Fearing the worst—a tumor—we took him to a specialist who examined him, took a few X-rays, did an MRI, and diagnosed him with lumbar spinal stenosis, a narrowing of the spinal canal in his lower back that resulted in the nerve root compression that was causing his sciatica. Better than a tumor, but still not good.

For months we tried to manage his symptoms with physical therapy, anti-inflammatory drugs, and special stretching exercises that he did on his bedroom floor, under the watchful eye of slightly perplexed Dr. Ting-Pei Warren. But these things brought little or no relief. We turned to steroid injections, "like the baseball players get," but they were painful and didn't help either.

It was around this time that Dad started showing signs of depression. His afternoon naps got longer and longer, and started earlier and earlier. My whole life, he had been meticulous about his appearance—shaving even on the weekends—but now several days of scruff consistently shadowed his face. Back when he was working, he used to set his clothes out the night before—socks, boxers, undershirt, dress shirt, and tie. Even after he retired, he still laid out the first three, with a carefully selected flannel or polo shirt, depending on the season. But lately he was puttering around in sweats and a T-shirt all day.

Other small habits were changing. Before going to bed, he used to put the filter in the coffee machine and scoop the dark roast into it so that all he had to do the next morning was push the button and, *voilà*. Now he just waited for Mom to make it. And he canceled his subscription to the Sunday *New York Times*. "Too much work," he said.

They were little things, and people do change; we weren't unduly alarmed. But taken together, they worried us. Somehow Dad just wasn't quite right. Ting seemed to sense it, too. Fewer cuddles from him, fewer kisses. He'd grow short with her when she meowed for attention, calling for Mom to make her stop. Ting was used to being the center of attention, and all of a sudden, Dad was.

Dad discussed his mood with his primary care physician during his annual physical, and the doctor prescribed an antidepressant, which Dad started taking without talking with me first. I believe that antidepressants are for people who want to be dead, not people who want to be happy—in other words, that they serve a purpose in the most severe cases, but should be a last resort. No doubt my opinion has been influenced by a book I was publicizing at the time, *The Depression Cure* by Dr. Stephen Ilardi, which advocated things like light therapy, dietary changes, exercise, and increased social interaction. I was angry at the doctor for taking what I saw as the easy way out—a shortcut that could forever alter my father's natural brain chemistry. I was angry at my dad for not consulting with me on something I saw as a major decision, and I was mad at my mom for going along with it, and for keeping his secret.

The antidepressant didn't work and, between it and all of the medicines he was taking for his heart and his back, my dad was having migraines and feeling nauseous all the time. I told him I thought his body was becoming toxic, and he and Mom agreed. We convinced the doctor to wean him off the antidepressant, and decided to refocus our efforts on relieving his back pain, which seemed to be the thing that depressed him the most.

As soon as we could get an appointment we took Dad to see a neurosurgeon, expecting him to recommend a laminectomy (a bone-removing spinal surgery that sounded scary, and which we weren't even sure Dad would be cleared for, given his heart condition). Instead, he suggested a relatively new procedure, called an X-stop. It involved minimally invasive surgery to implant a titanium spacer between two vertebrae. Everything Mom and I read about it said that it was a fairly quick procedure that patients generally tolerated well. We were even more encouraged by what the post-surgery data showed: X-stops worked. As if to prove it, the surgeon had Dad stand up straight and asked him how he felt. "Not good." Then he bent Dad forward just the slightest bit, and asked him again. "No pain." The spacer would alleviate the pressure that was causing the pain, just like bending him forward had done, but it would do so in such a way that Dad would have relief even when completely vertical.

Though he was in almost constant pain, Dad took a bit more convincing. He wasn't up for another surgery, another hospital stay. But then the doctor said the magic word: *outpatient.* Dad could be in and out the same day. In less than a week, the surgeon got clearance from Dad's cardiologist (who insisted on a stress test first, which, miraculously, Dad passed), and the procedure was scheduled.

I took the day of Dad's back surgery off of work. It was my job to change Ting's water and put down extra food; to do the driving and to bring Dad's various pills; to hold his glasses for him while he was in surgery and to keep track of his watch. We left the house around seven a.m., and by nine a.m. he was prepped and on his way to the OR. He was calm—much calmer than he'd been for his bypass—so Mom and I were calmer, too. After they wheeled him off to the OR, we went and grabbed tea in the hospital cafeteria, then camped out in the waiting area.

I did my best not to think back to Dad's bypass, but the situations were similar enough that I couldn't help it. The scary memories resurfaced—from the catheter they dropped through the side of his neck so they could monitor his blood pressure during surgery, to his sternum being cut in half and spread open so they could gain access to his heart; from the veins they harvested from his leg for the grafts, to how swollen he looked from all the IV fluids and blood products when we were finally escorted to the recovery room to see him; and finally, from the Streptokinase, a bacterial product they gave him through his IV to eat away at the postoperative adhesions that had formed in his heart, to how hard Mom and I pushed the doctors to have his breathing tube removed as soon as possible, while he was still kind of twilighty from the anesthesia, so that he wouldn't remember the feeling of being on a ventilator. I remembered Dad having hiccups nonstop for three full days after his bypass because his diaphragm had been irritated during surgery. It sounds funny, but it wasn't; hiccups hurt when your breastbone is held together with nothing but wire and you have half a foot of staples running down the middle of your chest.

Though my mind was working overtime to make it just as bad, this surgery was much less frightening than Dad's bypass had been. It was also considerably shorter. In a procedure that lasted a little over an hour, Dad's back pain went away for good. After a brief stay in Recovery and a final once-over by the surgeon, we got to bring Dad home.

I drove carefully, avoiding all the potholes on Pond Street. I took the speed bumps on Stillwater Circle extra slow. After pulling in the garage, I eased Dad out of the front seat, held him by the elbow while he walked upstairs to the bedroom, and helped him lower himself into his rocker. I tucked our fluffiest pillow behind his back and handed him the remote control and a giant bowl of vanilla-bean ice cream with chocolate sauce that Mom had scooped for him (he'd earned it), and left him to watch the Yankees game in comfort for the first time in over a year.

Except for a plum-colored bruise on his lower back and about an inch of stitches, you'd never suspect he'd just had surgery. His eyes were bright. He had energy. His appetite was back. He felt good. Mom offered him a post-op pain pill that the doctor had prescribed, and he waved it off with a quick "I don't need that crap."

Later that night, he picked Ting up and danced around the bedroom with her, cheek to cheek, while singing "Unchained Melody." He was finally happy again. We all were.

CHAPTER TEN

December 18, 2008

If human lives be,
for their very brevity, sweet,
then beast lives are sweeter still.

—ISOBELLE CARMODY

In the fall of 2008, not long after his back surgery, my father was diagnosed with myeloproliferative disease, a disorder in which excess cells are produced in the bone marrow. Mom and I researched it and learned that, in a matter of years—or months, if we weren't lucky—it would likely turn into leukemia. Dad knew the name of what he had and that it was serious, but he didn't know how it progresses. Mom and I didn't tell him. The doctors didn't tell him. He didn't know how to use Google, so he didn't know that the disease is sometimes referred to as "pre-leukemia." My father was a worrier by nature, and Mom and I were determined to do the worrying for him.

Weeks after his diagnosis, Dad started having a tingling sensation in his left arm. It was a symptom he knew well, and a feeling he hated. We took him to the emergency room of a nearby hospital, and they admitted him. Because his condition seemed so unstable, Mom and I slept in his room, in reclining chairs that the nurses wheeled in for us. He had tried to convince us to go home, but something told us not to leave him.

At some point in the middle of the night, Dad called out to us that he was feeling worse. We could see that he was sweating profusely—more than just the night sweats he'd been having lately, a telltale sign of myeloproliferative disease. Mom rang the call button for the nurse, who came in and took his pulse, his blood pressure, and his tempera-ture. His temperature was a bit elevated, but nothing else seemed out of whack to her. She gave him two aspirin, and told him to try to go back to sleep.

A half-hour passed, and he still didn't feel right. We saw that he was becoming increasingly agitated, and it was starting to worry us deeply. Mom gestured to a poster on the wall with a twenty-four-hour number patients or their family members could call if they felt they needed more care than they were getting—a number that would summon some sort of special support team.

"Should I dial it?" I whispered.

"Go to the nurses' station and threaten to," said Mom.

So that's what I did and, because by that point I was really scared, I was horribly rude. I lobbed phrases like "substandard care" and "inadequate action." I asked for supervisor names. Out of a genuine desire to help my dad, or a genuine desire to get me out of her hair, one of the nurses picked up the phone and dialed the hotline number herself.

To the hospital's credit, a mere five minutes later a three-person support team was in Dad's room hooking him up to an EKG. They said it didn't show anything out of the ordinary, and by the time they'd removed the leads from Dad's chest, he said he was feeling better. Shortly after they left, he fell asleep. Shortly after he did, Mom did.

I lay awake in the half-light of the hospital room the rest of the night, thinking that we had many more nights like this ahead of us—worse ones, probably. Probably much worse. There was no self-pity, just fear for my father and a sense of dread—and a helplessness I wasn't used to. My parents had gone out of their way to raise me to believe there was nothing I couldn't do, but I felt powerless to help my father. I had grown up thinking my way out of every bad situation, but I didn't know how to think his way out of cancer. All Mom and I could do was advocate for him, and surround him with good doctors.

I also thought about being an only child that night. Growing up, it was lovely. I don't recall ever feeling lonely— I had plenty of friends to play with, and Cinnamon, and Oregano. And Nonnie and Grampa too, of course. And Mom and Dad, who lavished me with attention. And I had my imagination to keep me company—a general store beneath the Ping-Pong table, full of rinsed-out yogurt containers, empty graham-cracker boxes, Styrofoam egg cartons, and Monopoly money for making change. Plus I had books— lots of books—to be with. Laura Ingalls Wilder and Anne of Green Gables were my friends. I read the whole Trixie Belden series—thirty-nine books—in a single summer.

But in the hospital that night, for the first time in my life, I wished I had a brother or sister—someone to stay with Mom and Dad while I went to fetch a nurse, or even just a cup of tea; someone to help me interpret the notes on the chart that hung on the wall by Dad's bed. Someone to tell me it would be all right. Maybe a husband could do these things, but I didn't have one handy.

It hit me that night that someday both Mom and Dad would be gone and that, when they were, I wouldn't have a family. That no one would remember "raccoon theater"— how we used to scatter marshmallows on the back lawn of our house in Ohio so that, after dark, we could turn off the inside lights, turn on the outside ones, and settle near the window to watch the raccoons enjoy their treat. That no one would remember how, at 11:11 every night, whichever one of us noticed it first would cry out "Happy our time!" simply because my father had designated it as such. That no one would remember the trip to Greers Ferry Lake where Dad dislocated his shoulder trying to get onto a raft, but where we found great barbecue afterward—pulled pork sandwiches with that vinegary sauce they have in Arkansas that Dad said was worth a little pain. That no one would remember the night I brought Ting home, and how I slept on the floor of my parents' room to help her transition from me to them. That no one would remember any of it. No one, that is, except me.

But all of these were selfish thoughts. I wanted—and needed—to focus on Dad.

The next morning, Dad's hematologist/oncologist came by. He wanted to do a bone marrow aspiration to get a better sense of how Dad's myeloproliferative disease was progressing. I had always thought such procedures were done in an operating room—too many episodes of *Grey's Anatomy* or *House*, I suppose—but he said he could do it right there, and summoned a nurse to help him. When she arrived with a tray of instruments draped in hospital-blue, Mom and I went out into the hall to wait. Five minutes later we heard Dad scream in pain. It was guttural, and cut us. Mom grabbed my arm as if to steady herself.

Seconds later, the door to his room opened and the nurse slipped out. She inched away from the room holding on to the wall, mumbling something about the size of the needle and feeling like she might faint. I ran for the nurses' station to get someone else to help Dad's doctor while Mom walked the nurse to the nurses' lounge.

A little while later the doctor came out. He pulled a small vial from the pocket of his lab coat and held it up to the light. It was filled with fluid, and what I think was a little piece of bone. "We'll send it to the lab," he said, "but if it were leukemia, it'd probably be cloudier. This is actually pretty clear." Encouraged that the myeloproliferative disease might at least be progressing slowly, Mom and I took a deep breath, gathered ourselves, and went back into Dad's room. He already had the TV on and was searching for a ball game. We said nothing about having heard him cry out or how incredibly brave he'd been, and he said nothing about how much the procedure had hurt him.

Before releasing him, Dad's doctors consulted and agreed that his angina was likely tied to the myeloproliferative disease. He was given a blood transfusion, and it seemed to do the trick; the angina lifted, and we got to take him home. Looking back, I suspect my father had a minor heart attack that night.

A few days later, on my mother's sixty-ninth birthday, my father wrote a letter to his cardiologist:

11/25/08

Dear Dr. C.,

Just to bring you up-to-date: After seeing you last Thursday I had my blood taken as you requested upstairs. I then went home and basically did nothing all day. The angina pain continued, and nitro abated it.

By Friday the rapidity of the left forearm attacks continued, and I finally went to the ER in the late afternoon, on Dr. Meow's advice.

My HCT was down to 24.5, and it was decided to start giving me a blood transfusion. Dr. McKurgi (can't spell his name) stopped in, and had a lot to do with the blood step-up. I wound up having four liters (pints?), and my HCT got up to 38.5. I was finally released on Sunday. Once the blood started I had no angina attacks, and started feeling better.

Dr. Sanz-Altamira, my oncologist, did a bone marrow biopsy while I was in the hospital—results pending; will keep you advised.

General consensus: It's the blood flow caused by the myeloproliferative disorder that is probably causing my problems.

Having the echocardiogram today as scheduled—the saga continues. I await your feedback on the blood work taken upstairs, as well as the echo.

The hopeful,
Jerry Warren

Dr. Meow was, in actuality, Dr. Miao—an Asian name—but my father heard it as any cat-parent would.

Several things about this letter were telling. By referring to Dr. Sanz-Altamira as his "oncologist" rather than his "hematologist," Dad showed more awareness of his illness than we realized. The careful tracking of his hematocrit numbers proved that he was still capable of being an active participant in his own care. And his salutation—"The hopeful, Jerry Warren"—showed how much he wanted to live. It's that last bit that still gets me.

About three weeks later, on the evening of December 17, Mom called me at work to tell me Dad was having angina again, and that she was taking him to the hospital. I grabbed my coat and my laptop and headed right for the car, realizing halfway there that I'd left my snow boots beneath my desk, but not wanting to take the time to go back for them.

Driving north I let my thoughts get the best of me. Worst-case scenarios flooded my mind. I kept the radio off in case my cell phone rang, and still glanced down at it every few minutes just to make sure I hadn't somehow missed a call when driving through one of the many dead zones along Route 93.

When I got to the emergency room forty-five minutes later, the tingling sensation in Dad's left arm was more severe than it had been when Mom first called me, and more severe than it had been during his previous hospital visit. Though he had walked in under his own power, it soon became clear that something was seriously wrong. The doctors, in the midst of a shift change, and quick to blame things on his myeloproliferative disease, didn't catch what was, in retrospect, blatantly obvious. One of them seemed unsure of how to work the EKG machine. Another one—completely lacking anything remotely resembling a bed-side manner—flew into the room and threw on the lights that Mom had dimmed so Dad could try to get some rest, and announced that they could try to give Dad some sort of clot-busting medicine, but that if there wasn't a clot, it could kill him.

As the evening wore on, no plan of action was put in place. No decisions were made on my father's behalf by anyone in a white coat, and Mom and I couldn't even tell which doctor was supposed to be making them. At one point, a nurse told him dismissively that he was "just having unstable angina" and would "have to learn to live with it."

Eventually the tingling crept into Dad's jaw, and from that point on the night is something of a blur. I remember running out to the nurses' station—literally running—to tell them his new symptom, half expecting them to hit some sort of giant red button that would immediately summon every doctor within a ten-mile radius. The nurse said that he was going to be admitted, and that someone would be right in to take him upstairs to intensive care, because the cardiac care unit was full.

Time elapsed; I couldn't say how much. Eventually, a tiny nurse came in to hook him up to a portable heart monitor. She explained that there was a ramp they'd have to go up, and that she'd need a running start for it. I remember me and Mom running along after the gurney, not wanting to leave Dad alone for a minute, not trusting that he was in capable hands. I remember Dad holding on to the gurney railings for dear life as it bounced its way up the impossibly long ramp with its impossibly steep angle for anything on wheels.

At the top of the ramp we boarded an elevator, and when it let us off on the intensive care floor, the nurse wheeled him into the unit, telling us to go sit in the waiting room while she got him settled in. For some reason I will never understand, Mom and I obeyed. Minutes later, a code blue was called, and we watched doctor after doctor run by. In ignorance or deep denial, we didn't put two and two together. Eventually, a woman in a white coat came out and told us that my father had had a massive coronary—right there in a hospital, with a state-of-the-art cardiac catheterization unit that they never used to try to save him.

My father hung on through the night. He regained consciousness briefly—long enough to squeeze my hand when I asked him if he could. They intubated him so that he could breathe, and they sedated him. They put salve in his eyes to keep them moist, because they were still half open. Mom pulled ChapStick from her purse, and smoothed it across his lips as best she could, taking care to avoid the tube.

Over a period of five or six hours, Dad coded so many times that I lost count. Mom and I stood at the foot of his bed each time, trying to give the doctors room to work, holding on to each other and telling Dad he'd be okay, even though we didn't think he could hear us—even though we didn't think he was going to get through this.

One of the nurses asked us if there was a family member we'd like to call.

"We're it," I snapped. "This *is* our family."

The nice nurse backed away.

Toward morning, the cardiologist on call—the same one who'd placed Dad's stent years earlier—came by. I asked him if we should look into MedFlighting Dad to a hospital in Boston—Massachusetts General, maybe. He said that he'd considered that, but didn't think Dad was stable enough to make it. Then he asked us if we believed in God. I told him we believed in *people*, though in my heart I knew that the ER doctors had failed my father, and that by allowing them to fail him, Mom and I had failed him too.

My father died shortly after seven a.m. on a cold and appallingly sunny Thursday. He was still warm when we kissed him good-bye.

CHAPTER ELEVEN

The Sock Drawer

"Name the different kinds of people," said Miss Lupescu.
"Now."
Bod thought for a moment. "The living," he said. "Er.
The dead." He stopped. Then, ". . . Cats?" he offered,
uncertainly.

—NEIL GAIMAN

After arranging for an autopsy, we left the hospital quickly.
I can't remember who drove—can't recall which car we
took or which streets we went down or what words we said,
if any. When we got home, Ting came to the top of the

stairs to greet us, like usual, but did a 180 when she didn't see Dad. That part I remember.

And so our life without Dad begins . . .

We set about making the necessary calls. First, Aunt Harriet—Dad's only sibling. Even though their father had died of a heart attack, and even though she'd had a triple bypass shortly after Dad's quadruple, she's still shocked by the news. She screams and hands the phone to Uncle Harold. Next, our Florida cousins, the Clays, with whom we spend most holidays and with whom my parents have taken many trips, including a quick but memorable one to Acadia National Park in Maine where they ate lobster bisque and fed a seagull pancakes. They are stunned as well. They express regret that they're so far away, and promise to come up soon.

We call Mom and Dad's longtime friends—Elliot and Sharon, Phyllis and Irv, Connie and Ted, and the ever-faithful Judy. We hold off on calling Dad's cousin, Ira, himself a cardiologist. We want to have a long talk with him—to go over the things that happened that night, and the things that should have happened but didn't. But we're not ready to go there yet.

I call in to work, tell one of the women in my department that my dad died, and that I'm putting on an "out of office" message. I e-mail my boss, telling him I'll come back to work as soon as I can, and that I don't know when that will be. I e-mail a couple of friends to cancel dinner plans for that night. They e-mail back to ask what they can do to help, but I can't think of anything. In fact, I can't actually think. I've been awake for more than twenty-four hours, and in one night I've lost half my family.

We hear our neighbor's garage door go up, and I walk out and tell Lyn what happened. Mom joins me, and they hug. Dad was friends with Lyn's husband, Bob. They used to play bridge together. Bob died of cancer a couple of years ago.

Later that day, Lyn cooks a whole chicken in a pot with jasmine rice, and brings it over to us. Our other neighbor, Charles, whom Lyn has alerted, stops by with his little girl, Samantha, to deliver turkey meatballs and couscous. We eat because we should. We eat, trying to ignore the empty chair—the one that didn't look out at the pond because my father wanted Mom and me to have the nicest view. In the spring, it's like a Monet out there.

But it's winter now, and everything is white. The birches by our brook are bent so low with snow that their foreheads are resting on the bank. The women in my department send flowers—a beautiful vase full of pine sprigs, baby's breath, and red roses, the latter of which we eventually dry and save. Days later, they send me a box with the Christmas presents they were planning to give me in person—a dark blue scarf and mitten set, a leather-bound day planner, a container of homemade oatmeal cookies. The only other box we receive contains my father's ashes, dropped off by Al, the funeral director, who doesn't push us when we say we won't be holding a service. Neither Mom nor I feel we could get through it, and we're certain Dad wouldn't want us to try.

The box is small and terrifyingly light, and we can't decide where to put it. We settle on Dad's sock drawer—the second drawer of his armoire, which we can see from the bed, and on which Ting likes to sleep, her face against the warm glass base of a squat heirloom lamp. We add his money clip and glasses. We add his watch. His wedding ring we put in the fireproof box we keep downstairs.

In ancient Egypt people were often buried with their cats, to keep them company in the afterlife. The cats received the same careful mummification as their humans—were wrapped in strips of linen and embalmed with fragrant spices. They were even afforded provisions for the journey: bowls of milk and mummified mice. If there's a Heaven, Dad's in it . . . but he's there without Ting, and there's nothing we can do about it.

We are glad we had Dad cremated. It's the only way we can keep him in the house with us—keep him in the room where he used to sit in his rocker, watching the Yankees on TV, his old blue robe around his shoulders, Ting nestled against his chest.

He was raised in an apartment building with a "no animals allowed" policy. All he had was a tank of tropical fish—mollies, guppies, the occasional neon tetra. And while he saw to it that I had what he did not have as a child—namely, a cat to cuddle—he also saw to it that I had a tropical fish tank. I loved that tank, and the responsibility that came with it, for I was in charge of alerting him when the pregnant fish were about to pop so he could put them in a separate container where their babies, once born, wouldn't be eaten. Unfortunately, on one occasion, a guppy got so pregnant it died—which led my father to fetch a razor blade and perform a delicate guppy C-section, saving all six fan-finned babies and stopping me from crying.

The apartment where Dad grew up was in the shadow of Yankee Stadium—a stadium that would hold its last inning a mere three months before he died. He had told me once that, when he couldn't fall asleep at night, he imagined himself as a Yankees pitcher—a closer from the dugout, called in to save the game. Just like I escaped into books, Dad escaped into baseball.

Christmas comes. We try to pretend it's just another day. We don't wrap the usual can of tuna fish for Ting. We watch *What Not to Wear* and other mindless shows on TLC—anything to distract us; any channel that doesn't have news breaks that contain decorated trees, wreathed front doors or, worse, a family around a table. Sometimes Mom nods off. She hasn't been sleeping well, and I know this because I have been sleeping in her bed—sleeping in my father's spot, just so it isn't empty.

I will sleep in my parents' bed for months. I will fall asleep at two or three a.m., and always with the TV on to save me from my thoughts. I will dream him dead again and again, each time a different way. I'm always there, but the common thread is I never manage to save him.

I also dream my father is a cat. Having read somewhere that Buddhists believe cats can act as hosts for human souls,

I imagine him in feline form being allowed into Heaven. He looks like Dusk, the tabby we fostered, and Heaven is our Ohio backyard, a long stone walkway with violets beside it, a hammock that he used to nap in.

Somehow Mom and I get through the holidays. I take the clothes I was wearing the night we lost him—a dark denim miniskirt, an old black T-shirt, a chartreuse cashmere cardigan, and my favorite pair of black tights—which have been lying for days on my bedroom floor, and stuff them in a plastic bag. They still smell like the hospital, but to wash or dry-clean them would seem too much like moving on. I bury the bag in my hamper. I cannot accept any of what has happened: that seventy-two years is all my father got, that all of us only get a little time here.

The autopsy results come back and show what we expected—a massive coronary. We need to obtain all of Dad's medical records—from the hospital, the hematologist/oncologist, and the cardiologist. All of the requests have to be made in person, which means Mom and I have to go to the hospital again—the last thing we want to do. Anxious, we get there too early and have to kill time in the cafeteria. Mom gets coffee and a bagel. Concerned there's too much cholesterol in cream cheese, I just get some tea. While I sip it, I keep an eye out for the doctors whom I hold responsible for Dad's death. I don't know what I'll do if I see them—glare, confront, avoid?

Thankfully I don't have to figure it out. Lots of white coats in here, but no one familiar.

We take the elevator to the fourth floor. The people in the hospital's records office are curt and officious. They make us fill out forms, and then charge us a fee. The head of the records department appears, and comes off to us as defensive, telling us it's unusual for a family to request the records of someone who's deceased. We don't believe him, but know better than to say it. We tell him just to be sure to give us *everything*. Then we take the elevator down to the hematologist/oncologist's office. When he learns we're there, he comes out to the waiting room to hug my mom and to tell her how much he liked my dad, and how the last time he saw him—the day before he died—he had a hunch the problem was unrelated to the myeloprolifera-tive disease, and that's why he had told my father to go see his cardiologist again. We don't get the sense he's trying to cover his ass. Like us, he seems full of regret.

Next we head to the cardiologist's office to get Dad's records. He invites us in and asks us to tell him what happened the night Dad died. I sum it up in ten words: "He was having a heart attack, and they missed it." He asks us who treated my dad that evening, and I tell him the doctors' names. The cardiologist knows one of them and tells us he's a good doctor, and a good man. I can't attest to the latter, but say "Apparently not" to the former. As we're leaving, we run smack-dab into the emergency room doctor. He's there to see the cardiologist—a social visit, it seems. I get the sense the two of them have each other's back.

On the way home, Mom and I go to Staples and make a copy of the records. Trying not to look at them, we box them up. It will be almost three years before we can gather the strength to send them to a law firm that specializes in medical malpractice—half hoping they'll take the case, half hoping they won't. If they do, it means a chance for justice for my dad. But it also means that they, too, suspect there was negligence involved. And if there was negligence involved, Mom and I were right there and allowed it to happen.

A few days later I head back to work, grateful for the distraction. I leave Ting in Mom's care, and Mom in Ting's.

Most days after work, I can make it as far as the garage elevator before I break down crying. And most nights I cry the whole way home, all forty-five minutes north. I'm still struggling to write my father's obituary—to come up with anything that remotely captures who he was. With Mom's help, I manage to complete it in time for what would have been Dad's seventy-third birthday—January 20, 2009. It's the day Barack Obama is inaugurated. I stream the ceremony on my computer at work, proud that Dad lived long enough to vote for him and see him elected, but sad he didn't get to see him sworn in.

My Father's Obituary

Jerome "Jerry" Warren of Salem, New Hampshire, died of a heart attack on December 18th. He was 72.

Born in the Bronx, he grew up playing stickball near Yankee Stadium and was a lifelong Yankees fan. He did, however, convert from the Giants to the Pats upon moving to the Boston area in the early 1990s. In addition to sports, he loved doing the Sunday New York Times *crossword puzzle, and rarely missed a letter.*

Upon graduation from New York's Dewitt Clinton High School, he entered the University of Michigan at the age of 16. After obtaining his degree, he served as a naval officer on the USS Grapple—*home-ported at Pearl Harbor—earning an Armed Forces Expeditionary Medal during the Matsu Islands Crisis. He went on to become a retail executive with Abraham and Straus, and later worked at Gimbels, the May Company, and Jordan Marsh.*

He enjoyed his retirement, traveling with his wife to China, Europe, Central America, Australia, Hawaii, and the Caribbean. While on safari in Africa, he kept a journal in which he noted every bird and beast they saw. But his favorite wildlife was on the pond in New Hampshire where they made their home. He constantly marveled at how a New York boy had come to love deer, otter, great blue heron, and hooded mergansers.

He was preceded in death by his father, Irving Warchaizer, and his mother, Pearl (Rappelfeld), as well as his in-laws, Grace and Michael, whom he loved. He is survived by his wife Donna (McKittrick) and his daughter Lissa, who liked the world more when he was in it, and are grateful that he knew. He also leaves his sister Harriet Silkowitz and her husband Harold, their daughters Paula and Adrienne, several close cousins, and a little gray cat named Ting, who still goes to see whose footsteps she's hearing, just in case they're his.

CHAPTER TWELVE

Spring and Summer

*I think that the world should be full of cats and full of
rain, that's all, just cats and rain, rain and cats, very
nice, good night.*

—CHARLES BUKOWSKI

Ting slowly adjusts to life without Dad. We all do. Because
he's not there to pal around with upstairs, she spends more
time on the window ledge on the lower level, napping in
the sun. Mom and I agree that she's sleeping more than
she used to—more than the thirteen to sixteen hours a day
that's normal for grown cats. We Google "cat depression."

It seems entirely plausible to me that Ting is depressed. In fact, it seems entirely plausible to me that a cat can have pretty much any emotion a human can. I reread a book I publicized, *Drawing the Line* by Steven Wise, in which he claims we know enough about the cognitive abilities of certain animals—bonobos, chimpanzees, orangutans, elephants, dolphins, African grey parrots, and dogs—that they should be afforded the same fundamental rights as humans: life, liberty, and the pursuit of happiness. Sounds a bit crazy until you learn that he was the first person to ever teach animal rights law at Harvard University. And until you really think about it.

Wise says the jury is still out on cats—that we haven't studied them enough yet to determine how much they can comprehend. It's just a matter of time, I say. One thing's clear: They grieve.

While Ting takes one approach, Mom and I take the other—going into overdrive. Mom busies herself as best she can. She goes to the market almost every day, though we have enough food to last us months. She makes all of the appointments she was loathe to make for herself when Dad was sick—eye doctor, dentist, hairdresser. She has the deck repainted, a new furnace installed, a bunch of chair cushions redone. She learns how to use an ATM because my father always gave her cash. I teach her to balance a checkbook, just like years before my father taught me: "To the penny, Lissa. To the penny." She switches Ting, who is thirteen now, to Eukanuba for seniors, and clips Ting's nails like it's religion. She brushes Ting so often that she starts to give off light.

One thing Mom *doesn't* tackle is the box of photographs beside her bed—the ones she'd been planning to sort through for an album. There are too many memories in that box, too many shots of Dad. It's just too soon to comb through them. I wonder if there are pictures of him and Ting. There must be a few; they were with each other so much. But I can't say we made a point of taking shots of them together. Simply put, we thought we had more time.

In January, I start teaching again—a graduate course on book publicity that I developed for the Writing, Literature, and Publishing program at Emerson College, a school that hugs the Boston Common. It meets every Thursday for an exhausting three hours and forty-five minutes. It always takes some adjusting to at the beginning of the semester—takes me a good two or three weeks to build up my stamina so that I can get through the class on just one cup of tea and without losing my voice. But this semester it seems physically harder. Even the T ride, from Kendall Square on the Red Line to Boylston on the Green Line, seems formidable, although it's a mere three stops and just involves one change of train.

I jostle for a seat, but it's rush hour, so I'm left to straphang. I feel like every stranger on the subway should know that my father died last month—should magically stand up and offer me their seat as a condolence, or just as mercy. No one does, of course. No one knows. They're not aware that he's gone, or that he was good, or that my body feels heavy. My twelve students are equally in the dark, which is a blessing and a curse—a curse because it's hard to be animated, hard to fake it for four straight hours; a blessing because, at least while I teach, my mind is otherwise occupied. My classroom becomes my safe room.

February comes, and my Raynaud's kicks into gear. If I'm outside for more than a few minutes, even if I have my gloves on, my fingers start to hurt and turn white, like little attacks of frostbite. It can result in nerve damage, though, so it can't be taken lightly. It's the reason my father had my car equipped with an automatic starter shortly after I was diagnosed my freshman year of college—so that, with the click of a button, I could turn it on from wherever I was to give it a chance to warm up.

I'm reminded of him every time I start the engine—not just because he bought me the automatic starter, but because, when I was little and we were living in Ohio (years before automatic starters existed), he used to go out in the cold and the lake-effect snow to turn over the car ten minutes before it was time to drive me to school so that it would be warm by the time I got in it.

Now, every time I go somewhere, I'm at once reminded of how much he loved me, and of the fact he's not around to take care of me anymore. He's not around to take care of Mom, either. That's my job now, and I don't think I'm very good at it. I buy her cupcakes for Valentine's Day just so she has something from someone—a dozen lemon-vanilla ones with strawberry frosting. Dad would have known her preference (chocolate cupcakes with chocolate frosting). She tells me gently, so I'll know for next time.

In March, Mom and I go on a cleaning tear. We decide that the seashells on the étagère in the living room are dusty, and spend a whole Saturday taking them down, one by one, brushing them off with old unmatched socks that we've turned into mittens, and polishing them with baby oil until they practically glow. There are hundreds and, between the two of us, we're able to remember who found most of them, and where: the keyhole limpets I located between rocks in Green Turtle Cay, the giant conch Mom literally tripped over at low tide in the Caymans, the cowries Dad dove for while snorkeling off Maui, and the tusk shell he bought in Sanibel for me because they're just too fragile to find along the beach. It's the most we've talked about Dad since his death, and because it hurts it will be the last we speak of him for weeks, so as not to risk upsetting each other. The house has grown so quiet that we can hear Ting's footsteps.

April, and the snow has crushed the crocuses—the dark purple ones in the park I walk through to get to my office each day. In prior years I bent down and wiped them off, but this year the cold seems colder, so I keep walking.

Always something of a workaholic, I let my job become my life. I tell myself that, given what my family has been through recently, it's a normal and acceptable response—more productive, say, than drinking. But the truth is, working is much easier than living, even when I have to lay off an assistant I practically raised from a pup. The truth is all calls don't have to be returned before I let myself have lunch, all paperwork doesn't have to be filed before I head home at night, and my in-box doesn't have to be empty of e-mail before I let myself go to bed. I know I'm being neurotic, but I don't know how to stop. I confide in a colleague who recently lost her dad, and she suggests I see a psychologist. Some of my craziest authors have been shrinks. I wave off her idea.

It's harder, though, to wave off the pains I'm having— or think I'm having—in my left arm. Going to a doctor is out of the question, as I've completely lost faith in them. Besides, it's classic psychosomatic behavior. I tell myself I'm fine, but should take this as an opportunity to change my diet for the better. I start snacking on walnuts and almonds—ten at a time, exactly ten. I eliminate red meat and egg yolks. Then I eliminate meat in general. I consult my company's myriad vegan cookbooks, and though the health benefits are undeniable, I decide I'd starve to death because it's hard to go vegan if you mostly just know how to bake. I consider, and dismiss, learning how to really cook. Too. Much. Effort. I start downing instant oatmeal like it's going out of style. I start taking a multivitamin, and a fish-oil supplement. I consider taking up jumping rope—something I used to love as a child, something that would be good for me now. But I'm afraid I'll have a heart attack while jumping. I decide to leave well enough alone.

Soon it's May, and no one at work seems to notice I'm half-cracked, which is good, except it's lonely. My authors continue to demand the usual attention: book tours, media, praise. My colleagues continue to demand results, and I continue to get them. I book an author on the *Today* show, and train it to Manhattan to escort him to the studio. When I get back, I score him three national NPRs, even though the shows normally compete. I convince C-SPAN's *Book TV* to tape another author's talk. I secure a review in the *New York Times Book Review*, another in *USA Today*, and land a book on the *New York Times* bestseller list—by the skin of its teeth, but it makes it. I'm nuts, but no one's the wiser: On the outside, things are status quo. Nothing feels good or normal, though. I'm on autopilot.

A robin builds a nest in the tree outside my office in one frenetic day, then decides not to use it—or finds she has nothing to fill it with. Most of the time I feel empty, too, and I'm becoming equally manic. I'm working every waking moment. Ting is the only thing I'll stop for. Holding her is the best part of my day.

Sometimes I wonder how Ting would react if Dad walked into the room. I have no doubt she'd remember him, but I don't think she'd go to him—at least, not right away. In cat years, six months is an awfully long time to be gone. He'd have to earn her forgiveness first.

But of course there will be no reunion, joyful or reserved. I'm not sure of the extent to which cats can understand death, but I know they can feel absence. And right now that's pretty much where I'm at when it comes to the subject of acceptance. Dad's death as a permanent state is beyond my comprehension.

In June, the lilac bush I gave my mom for Mother's Day years ago—the one Dad dug up, transported, and replanted when we moved to New Hampshire—blooms in its reliable way. I cut some branches and put them in a vase on the kitchen table, knowing they remind Mom of her parents, who had a row of lilacs along the fence in their backyard. I remember my grandparents' lilacs, too, from summers spent with them before we lost them—Nonnie first, then Grampa a decade later. I remember being a family of five, remember saying the number when giving our name at a restaurant reception desk. No one asks anymore. They look from me to Mom, and write "two."

Nonnie liked cats and cats liked her; in fact, her lap was Cinnamon's favorite. But Nonnie was also a bit wary of them. She would shoo Cinnamon off the dinner table and the kitchen counters, terribly afraid that cats spread germs. And yet, she was far more comfortable around cats than her own mother had been. My great-grandmother Katherine, who died many years before I was born, believed a cat could steal a baby's breath, and never let one near a crib. For some reason, she still kept cats in her home, though.

On a cold March day in 1984, when we were living in a western suburb of Cleveland, Nonnie died of renal failure. I was eleven. I remember three things from that day: the garage door going up too soon for visiting hours at the hospital to be over; my grandfather walking into the house with his shoulders so weighed down with grief that I thought he must have suitcases in his hands; and my mother taking me to a department store to buy a dress for Nonnie's funeral. The dress we chose was the color of lilacs, but I didn't make the connection until many years later.

My father accompanied my mother and me to upstate New York for Nonnie's funeral, but he didn't attend the interment. He had a bad cold, but I have my doubts that it was bad enough to warrant missing the burial. The truth is, I don't think he could bear it. The idea of putting my grandmother in the cold Fort Edward soil, and leaving her there, was something he couldn't process. He had loved my mother's mother like she was his own.

He felt the same way about my grandfather, who moved in with us shortly after Nonnie's death. Grampa was a man of few words, a former prison guard who was still strong and imposing well into his eighties. He had a soft spot for

Cinnamon, though, and I would often come home from school to find bits of his lunch beside her food dish.

Grampa died on my mother's fifty-third birthday. I was home from college on Thanksgiving break. We were celebrating at the kitchen table and I thought he was bending down to reach a dropped napkin, but his body just kept going, landing with such force that it knocked out his dentures and sent his glasses sliding across the floor. While my mother called 911 and my father ran to turn on all the outside lights so the ambulance could find the house, I knelt beside Grampa and tried CPR, which I'd learned years prior in a babysitting class. I didn't hear his ribs crack, but I remember feeling them give. When his lips blued I was sure that I had bruised them. In my last memory of him, he tastes like birthday cake.

June 18 is the six-month anniversary of my father's death, and because he was a man who celebrated half-birthdays, the date seems somehow momentous. I try to come up with a decent way to mark it. Because he wasn't Catholic, going to church to light a candle like my grandfather used to do for my grandmother doesn't seem quite right. Neither does sending a check to "Our Lady of Angels" like my mother does for her parents on their birthdays and the anniversaries of their deaths, so that masses will be said in their honor. And of course there's no grave to visit. It's then that I remember what my father used to do when he visited my grandparents' grave—place a pebble on their headstone, in the old Jewish tradition. I go outside and find the prettiest stone I can, and when Mom isn't looking, I put it in his sock drawer. Ting hears the drawer open and looks up from her nap.

June is normally pie time, because it's when the strawberries come in. The summer before Dad died they were unusually plentiful at our local farmers' market, and Mom made almost a dozen of her strawberry rhubarbs—the ones with the tapioca mixed in—because she knew it was his favorite. That fall she made his second favorite, sour cream apple, practically once a week, using Granny Smiths from nearby Mann Orchard. She felt good he'd had the foods he liked best the last year of his life.

But this summer there's no pie, no fried green tomatoes or ears of fresh corn. Not even on my birthday, which we agree to treat like any other day.

On the Fourth of July, Mom and I settle on the couch with a bowl of cherries between us and watch the Esplanade festivities on TV. As the Boston Pops plays "The 1812 Overture," the fireworks flood the screen—a brittle star, a lion's mane, a weeping willow. They're good, but we're indifferent. We could do without the drama. In fact, we'd prefer that nothing more explode, because everything already seems to be in pieces. Mom cracks the window to see if the air has cooled enough that we can turn off the AC.

By mid-July, the loosestrife and Queen Anne's lace and goldenrod have filled the banks of the brook in our backyard—the brook where our neighbor, Charles, scattered his father's ashes a decade ago, and Zulu's ashes last year. "A lot of good people in that creek," he had told my father once. But my dad remains in his sock drawer. We just can't let him go.

August arrives, and it's a hot one. Ting pancakes herself on the bathroom tiles every chance she gets. I hold my hands under the faucet and run them over her body to cool her, starting behind her ears and dragging down past her haunches. She normally hates getting wet, but seems grateful. Mom makes a giant batch of pasta salad, and we eat it for a week because it's just too hot to cook. We take turns filling the big glass pitcher with bottled water and bags of black tea, tenting it with tinfoil before setting it on the porch to brew. The three of us—me, Mom, and Dad—used to eat dinner on the porch in the summer, but we don't do it this year because we are two, not three, which makes it somehow not worth the effort to walk the distance from the kitchen to the deck. Baseball games—the background music to our summers and, somehow, to my childhood—are strangely absent. I catch myself hoping the Yankees are having a good season, and catch myself hoping they're not. If they win the pennant and Dad isn't here to see it, it would be unbearable.

Everything reminds me of loss this summer. Things that should make me happy—fresh peas to shuck, sun tea with lemon, falling asleep with the windows open—are irrelevant and irreverent. The swallows swooping above the pond, so close to the water they're like stones being skipped, don't even do it for me. My favorite things depress me, and the world doesn't know enough to stop being beautiful.

CHAPTER THIRTEEN

Ting Is Sick

Life is life—whether in a cat, or dog or man. There is no difference there between a cat or a man.

—SRI AUROBINDO

It's a Sunday morning in early September—cold enough that we put the heat on for a bit to take the chill off the house, and open every blind in an effort to let in the sun. The leaves on the maples are threatening to change, and the birches have already started surrendering. Warblers dart from tree to tree. They just arrived last week, and soon they'll finish migrating south. Like everything, they're temporary.

Dad loved the pond at this time of year, and it's our first fall without him.

I'm up in Mom's room with Ting, who doesn't seem like herself. Normally she'd be sprawled in the slant of light that falls across the couch at this hour, but today she's crouched on the floor in a shadow. I go over to her and drag my nails along both sides of her jawbone, but get no licks in return. In fact, she shifts away from me. I take the cushion off the orange armchair and put it on the floor for her. She looks at it, but doesn't move. I pick her up and put her down on it, and go sit on the bed to watch her. Maybe her stomach's upset. She must have gobbled her food again.

Less than a minute later she falls fast asleep, and rolls off the cushion and onto the carpet. The tumble wakes her. It's almost comical, except she's not a klutzy cat—and she's swaying back and forth now, almost like she's drunk.

I call Mom to come upstairs, and the urgency in my voice makes her decide not to argue, even though she's busy making us tea. When she hits the landing, I tell her what just happened—push her toward Ting, who is sitting on her haunches now, very, very still. Mom assesses the situation with a glance in my direction and decides I've gone batty. Reassuring me with a "Cats do that sometimes," she heads back downstairs with a shrug. Cats *do* sometimes do that—but not our graceful, dignified Ting. My mind immediately starts racing to the worst.

I go down a mental list of poisons she could have ingested. Poinsettia? No, too early in the year. Some kind of cleaning product? Unlikely—we've been slobs as of late. Some sort of toxic mold or mildew? Doubt it. I boot up my laptop and Google "feline fainting spell." Just one entry. Damn. I click on it, and see words like *leukemia* and *degenerative myelopathy*. I don't click the hyperlinks—too scary.

Before I exit out of the screen, I see that human medication is sometimes the cause. I go to the bottle of Valium Mom's been keeping beside the bed, but the cap is on tight. I get down on my hands and knees, half expecting to find a half-dissolved tablet next to her slippers, but all I find is a Ting toy—a green pipe cleaner coiled like a pig's tail. It's all I can do not to cry.

A few minutes later Mom comes back with the tea. I'm sitting on the edge of the bed, staring at Ting, who is still sitting on the floor, staring into space.

"How is she?" Mom asks.

"Still not right," I answer.

Mom hands me my cup and goes over to Ting, who of course flops immediately onto her side and stretches herself out in a glorious swan dive. She yawns, licks her paw, and rubs her face. Mom leans over and pets her head, and Ting-Pei starts to purr. I can hear it from across the room.

I'm an idiot.

Then Mom gets down on all fours and kisses Ting between the ears—five, six, seven times—before going into the bathroom to do her makeup and curl her hair. I reach for the *New York Times Book Review,* and lose myself in it until the fourth or fifth review, when Mom whispers my name. I look up to see her watching Ting walk toward her food dish. Ting takes two steps. Stops. Three steps. Sits. Two more steps, and she crouches down. Mom looks at me, and I look at her. Ting topples over like a too-full bag of groceries.

Moments later, Ting comes to and walks away like nothing happened. We're shaken, though, and debate whether we should take her to our vet's emergency room, because the regular part of the animal hospital is closed on Sundays. A little unsure of exactly what we saw, not wanting to put her through the stress of a vet visit unnecessarily, and thinking the doctor who knows her best won't be there on the weekend anyway, we decide instead to take turns watching her.

"Maybe it's just a virus," I offer. "Like a twenty-four-hour flu."

"Maybe," says Mom. It doesn't reassure me.

"I don't think it's a stroke," I say. "Or a heart attack." The last two words hang there, and I wish I hadn't said them.

"No, not that," Mom says after a pause. "She seems fine now."

But she's not fine—not by a long shot. By sunset she has had three more episodes. Twice she loses consciousness completely; once, she's just woozy and stumbles.

I take the first overnight shift, midnight to three. Ting sleeps through most of it—snoring, softly—but gets up once to use the litter box and lap a little water. When she's done, I pick her up and stuff her in Old Bluey, the robe I've had since she was a kitten. I walk around the room with her like that, trying to avoid the creaky parts of the floor, her little head peeking out from beneath the checkered polar fleece. I know when I hold her against my chest it's not sturdy and strong like Dad's was. I know I can't offer her what he provided—that solidity, that safety.

Around three a.m. on Monday morning I wake Mom to take over. Though she officially has the three-to-six shift, I get up at five, too nervous to sleep, and go make us English muffins. I'm extra generous with the strawberry jam in an attempt to make up for our lousy night—and the lousy day I'm quite sure we'll be having.

Two hours later our car is idling in the parking lot of the animal hospital while we wait for the reception desk lights to go on. Ting will be our vet's first patient, although we have no appointment. We've learned the hard way that, when it comes to the health of those you love, you can't afford not to be pushy.

When we enter the lobby things are already bustling even though we're the only patients there. An assistant is restocking the shelves with fifty-pound bags of dog food and hypoallergenic cat litter. Files for the day's patients are being pulled by the desk manager. Another assistant is wiping down the giant scale where they weigh the really big dogs. There's hot water standing ready on the counter, and Mom makes us some tea while I get settled with Ting in a corner where it's fairly quiet. We've covered her cat carrier with her favorite pale-yellow towel—for warmth and familiarity, and so she can feel hidden. When I lift a corner and peek at her through the slats, she sniffs the air, trying to identify all the strange smells, but doesn't make a sound.

Before the tea has time to brew, a woman with short gray hair and a long white coat comes over to greet us and escort us to the exam room. Dr. Belden is our longtime vet at Bulger Veterinary Hospital in nearby Andover, Massachusetts. She knows her stuff—every test, every procedure, and every medication under the sun, including ones for humans that have been proven safe and effective for animals in small dosages. We love her for her brain, but even more for her compassion.

Dr. Belden examines Ting with her trademark gentle manner, stopping occasionally to pet her, and speaking to her directly at times. We tell her about Ting's odd behavior—the tumbling and the fainting spells, their duration and frequency. She asks if Ting is eating like normal, takes her to the scale and weighs her. Seven pounds, ten ounces—about the same as her last checkup. Good. She looks in Ting's eyes with a light while I hold her, palpates her abdomen, checks her teeth and ears. Ting is very brave as blood is drawn from her left front leg. Then Dr. Belden listens to Ting's heart while staring at her watch, looks puzzled, and listens and times it again. "It's slow," she says. "Slow, like a dog's heart. I'd like to get an EKG."

Mom and I look at each other. "Should we tell her?" Mom asks me, and I nod yes.

"Karen, Jerry died this past winter. He had a heart attack. So whatever you think is wrong with Ting, we need you to fix it."

While Mom is at the front desk scheduling the EKG appointment, Dr. Belden takes Ting for an X-ray. It shows nothing alarming—no mass near her heart, no buildup of fluid, no shadow or enlargement. When she hands Ting back to me, she says, "Just keep an eye on her." She knows us well, and knows we will.

"I'm sorry about your dad," she says, while scratching Ting behind the ears.

"Thanks," I say. "We miss him."

It's then that I remember she too lives alone with her mom.

I-495 is the quickest way home. It takes us past the dealership where Dad got his Honda, the movie theater where he saw *Apollo 13*, the Friendly's we know he used to sneak off to for chocolate milkshakes with strawberry ice cream, and the hospital where they let him die. If it weren't for Ting I'd take back roads, just to avoid driving by it.

Ting's in the backseat, her cat carrier belted in. She doesn't make a peep. We get her home, thinking to enter by the front door so the grating sound of the garage door doesn't scare her. When we get to the foyer and unlatch the door to her carrier, she steps out of it gingerly. I scoop her up and carry her upstairs to Mom's room, figuring that having a cat with a really slow heartbeat try to make it two flights under her own steam wouldn't be a good idea.

Then Mom and I set about cat-proofing her room. We position pillows and wadded-up blankets against every hard surface, every coffee table leg and dresser corner that Ting could possibly knock into if she passed out. We move her water glass from the bathroom counter to the bathroom floor. She makes a beeline for her kitty bed on top of Dad's armoire, but we've already placed it on the couch—a softer, lower surface that we worry may still be too high. I scoop her up again and put her in it.

Ting settles in and starts cleaning herself. She begins with her two front legs, licking all the way down them in long, swift strokes. Next she licks her paws and draws them smoothly and efficiently across her head. Then it's on to her chest and belly—little licks this time, just flicks of the tongue. And finally, she reclines and lifts one of her back legs over her head; not exactly ladylike, but you have to admire the flexibility. Nothing about her actions says "sick cat."

Her EKG is set for Thursday morning. The days pass, eventless. As soon as five p.m. rolls around each day, I leave the office and head right home to relieve Mom from her cat-sitting duties. I get takeout from our nearby Thai place three nights in a row so that Mom can stay upstairs with Ting instead of being down in the kitchen, cooking. I try to tempt Ting with a shrimp from my Pad Thai, but she has never been that into people food, and turns her nose up at it. The fact that it's food from her native country is lost on her.

Ting seems to be doing so well that we start to question whether there's actually anything wrong with her at all. I Google how fast a dog's heart beats: 60 to 100 beats per minute for large dogs, up to 140 for small. I Google the normal heart rate for cats: 120 to 200. According to Dr.

Belden, Ting came in at a mere 65, and 60 is considered the fainting zone. It's hard to ignore the numbers, but, of course, I'm in denial. I decide Dr. Belden must have measured wrong, and set about taking Ting's pulse myself. I feel for it on her wrist like you'd do with a human, but I can't find it there. Complicating this attempt, Ting curls her paws around my fingers and licks me. Then I search for it on her neck, which she interprets as a preamble to a nice hard scratch, and bites me lightly when I don't deliver. It's hopeless; I can't even find her pulse, much less get an accurate reading. We'll have to be patient, and we'll have to take her in for the test.

At 6:45 that Thursday morning we coax Ting into her cat carrier for her 7:00 a.m. appointment. When we get to Bulger, we go to the back entrance as instructed. A staff member ushers us right into an exam room, where the technician is already set up. He introduces himself while Mom and I undo the plastic pegs of Ting's carrier so that we can just lift off the top. The technician is big and has a booming voice, and we know there's no way Ting will come out the door for him like she did for Dr. Belden earlier that week.

He positions Ting on her side and proceeds to squirt her with alcohol—for better conduction, he explains—using the kind of long-nozzled bottle football players use when they're wearing their helmets. Ting doesn't like it one bit, but shows tolerance. While I stroke her head the technician affixes clamps to her belly and chest. They look like miniature jumper cables but don't seem to hurt her—or perhaps she's just too scared to show it. Once they're all in place, the technician asks Mom, who's standing next to the switch, to turn off the overhead lights, and then he pushes a button on his computer. Ting's heartbeats spread across the screen like stalagmites. Mom and I both look away. We've seen enough of these readings this year.

The room is unnaturally quiet; no bleeps or blips accompany the readout, just the sound of our breathing. Almost immediately he identifies the problem: second-degree AV block. We know bypasses, grafts, and stents. We know arterial stenosis and cardiac catheterization. We surmise that AV means "atrioventricular." We know the language of heart disease, but this "AV block" is a new one for us.

"What is that?" Mom asks.

We're told in layperson's terms that the electrical impulses in one part of Ting's heart aren't making it to the other; that means it's not receiving instructions to pump, which is why she has become "syncopal." I turn the word around in my head. As an English major, I learned it referred to sounds or letters left out of the middle of a word—in-*ter*-est-ing pronounced in-*trest*-ing instead. But to doctors, it means a loss of consciousness caused by lack of blood to the brain. I like my definition better. I don't want to be here.

"What causes AV block?" Mom asks. We're told it could be due to aging, or a type of heart muscle disease called cardiomyopathy.

It's good to have a diagnosis, but it's a frightening-sounding one. Cutting to the chase, Mom asks the technician how it's treated—if Ting will have to be on some sort of medication for the rest of her life. He tells us Dr. Belden will explain the options. *Good,* we think. *There are options.*

We blot Ting off with paper towels as best we can, put her back in her carrier, and take her to the lobby to wait while Dr. Belden pores over the EKG results. About fifteen minutes later we're escorted into another exam room. Soon after, Dr. Belden comes in, looking more serious than I have ever seen her.

"I'm referring you to Angell Animal Medical Center in Boston," she says. "They're one of the few places in the country that have successfully implanted a pacemaker in a cat."

CHAPTER FOURTEEN

Monitoring

Time spent with a cat is never wasted.

—COLETTE

The cat with five hearts needs a new one—or, rather, an engine for her old one.

The following Monday I chauffeur Ting to Angell. It's an hour's drive from home, most of it highway. We transport her in her cat carrier, seat-belted into the driver's-side backseat, and positioned so that the front door faces the passenger-side backseat, where Mom sits so she can keep an eye on Ting and soothe her as necessary.

To get to Angell, we have to pass through the Longwood Medical Area, home to Brigham and Women's Hospital and Beth Israel Deaconess Medical Center; home to Dana-Farber Cancer Institute and the Joslin Diabetes Center. Even just being near a hospital makes me nervous after what happened to Dad, but I don't say anything, and Mom doesn't either. I don't say I wish we'd brought him to a Boston hospital instead.

We pull into the parking lot at Angell and see dogs being walked by people in scrubs: a dachshund waddling in a front-leg cast; a German shepherd trotting with gauze wrapped around his belly; a shih tzu or Lhasa apso (I can never tell the difference) propelling himself forward at a pretty good speed, even though his hind legs are in some sort of wheelchair contraption; a golden retriever who looks perfectly healthy but who walks with so much hesitance, I wonder if he's blind. I find a spot near the sliding-glass front door, park, and pop out so I can unbuckle Ting's carrier. She doesn't make a peep—wants to remain invisible.

The lobby of Angell is impressive—as big as that of any human hospital. The waiting area is thoughtfully sectioned off for dogs, cats, and "other," which I assume means rabbits, ferrets, and guinea pigs, perhaps the occasional sugar glider or other small exotic. While Mom goes and checks us in, I hunker down in the "cats" section, Ting's carrier on my lap with her pale-yellow towel draped over the top, just the way she likes it.

After a few minutes, we're greeted by a young woman who introduces herself as Sara, the cardiology assistant. She brings us back to an exam room. I open the door to Ting's carrier to see if we can coax her out. No dice, of course—new place, new people—so one by one I undo the plastic pegs that hold the case in place, remove the cover, hand it to Mom, and lift Ting out. She's too scared to meow in protest. The room is very bright and smells of antiseptic.

Sara pulls out a scale on which I set Ting. Seven pounds, ten ounces—just like at Dr. Belden's. Then, while Mom holds Ting in her arms and sways back and forth with her like she did with me when I was a baby, we answer a bunch of questions. Is she eating normally? Yes. Any bathroom problems? No. Vomiting? Occasionally, when she scarfs her food—the usual cat throw-up stuff. Is she on any medication? No. How long has she been fainting? First time was last week. How many spells since then? Exactly three. What happens when she faints? She goes out cold and falls. How long is she out? Just seconds.

The basics covered, we chat with Sara while we wait for the cardiologist to arrive. It turns out Sara recently graduated from Emerson with a degree in creative writing. She rattles off the names of professors with whom she studied, and I nod my head; I know all of them. The school is well respected for its liberal arts program—with emphasis on the *liberal*—and I'm surprised to find someone who studied there working in the medical field. I like her instantly for being different; plus, she was gentle with Ting.

The door opens, and a white-coated Dr. Nancy Laste, the "cat cardiologist," walks in, followed by a couple of white-coated interns. Like the places we passed on the way here, this is a teaching hospital.

Mother of three (including newborn twins, we later find out), Dr. Laste is head of the cardiology department, having obtained her veterinary degree from Cornell University. She exudes competence and confidence and, after looking over Ting's chart, listening to her heart for what seems like ages, and asking us a bunch more questions, she declares Ting an excellent candidate for a pacemaker. She tells us that cats with pacemakers generally live to whatever age they would have lived to without heart block.

We're encouraged, but still, we ask a zillion questions: Is she certain a pacemaker is necessary (yes); at fourteen, is Ting too old for the operation (not if she's otherwise healthy, no); how long will Ting have to stay in the hospital (a week at most); will she be able to feel it each time the pacemaker fires (no); how long will the pacemaker last (long enough). But it's her answer to our last question that scares us. "When's the last time you've successfully paced a cat?" Her response: "Probably ten years ago."

Seeing our faces, she goes to a drawer and pulls out a metal disk wrapped in plastic and sets it on the table. "We do them all the time for dogs," she says. "Just not so much for cats." Looking at the size of the pacemaker, it's easy to see why—and hard to imagine the thing actually fitting inside Ting, much less the intricate stitching it'd take to attach the giant device to her heart. It's the size of a silver dollar, and at least ten times thicker.

"You'd use a smaller one for Ting, right?" asks Mom. "They make them smaller for cats?"

"It's one size fits all," says Dr. Laste. "Same for dogs and cats and humans."

It's then that we realize Ting will be receiving a *human* pacemaker. Apparently, the demand for animal-size pacemakers isn't such that any company would find it lucrative enough to produce them.

Mom lifts the pacemaker off the table and puts it in her palm, weighing it as if it were a piece of fudge. She hands it to me and we look at each other, both of us thinking *This is crazy*, but knowing we have no other option—knowing that any one of Ting's fainting spells could be fatal. We don't need to discuss it. Ting deserves to live. We're going to proceed, despite the odds. We've lost enough this year.

To know how to pace her properly, Dr. Laste needs to get a recording of one of Ting's episodes. She tells us Ting will need to stay overnight with a heart monitor in place.

They take her away to attach the sensors and hook them up, then allow us to go back and see her. She's miserable, and scared. They have her in a large ground-floor cage, with dogs on either side of her. The walls between them are solid so she can't see them, but no doubt she can smell them and hear them panting.

I see a woman a few cages down who has crawled into the cage with her Chihuahua. Seeing me look at her, she simply says, "They'll let you get in, too." I hand my purse to Mom and undo the latch, gingerly sliding myself in so as not to disturb Ting. She tries to stand up but is wobbly and tethered. I pick her up and place her against my chest, wrapping her in my cardigan. She nestles against me and settles a bit, but there's too much going on for her to sleep. It's cramped in here, and after a few minutes my feet go numb. All I can do is let them.

When the visiting hour is over, I place Ting on the blanket they've given her and extricate myself from the cage. I glance back at Ting, and she's shaking. I look at Mom, but don't have to say anything. This time, when we don't like how things are being handled at a hospital, we're going to speak up. Mom informs the nurse that we'll be taking Ting home with us, and asks for her to be disconnected. There has to be a better way.

And thankfully, there is. Hearing we're determined to spring Ting from the joint, Dr. Laste comes by and fits her with a portable heart monitor—an "event monitor," they call it—the same kind that people with suspected heart problems wear clipped to their waistband or belt; the same kind that my father wore once. For Ting, of course, the only option is to cover her midsection with gauze and then wrap the gauze with a special, self-adhesive bandage (appropriately named "pet wrap") so that the monitor can be affixed to her back. The pet wrap is bright green, and the second the monitor is clipped to it, Mom turns to me and says "Jet pack." Indeed, Ting looks like Boba Fett from *Star Wars.*

Armed with instructions for operating the monitor, we settle up at the front desk and head to the car. Ting is still and quiet the whole way home. As soon as we get her upstairs, she makes it her mission in life to rid herself of the dreaded device, thrashing about in an effort to shake it loose. But Mom and I make it our mission to keep the darn thing on her. Every time she tries to jump off the bed, or into the rocker where she loves to nap, or onto the sink, we scoop her up and gently put her wherever she was trying to go. To further complicate matters, one of us has to be with her at all times so that, in the event she has an episode, we can push the RECORD button on the top of the monitor so that it commences taping, then call the 800 number for the monitoring service and hit TRANSMIT. The sooner we capture an incident, the sooner she can have her surgery. The sooner she can be well.

Mom and I develop a routine. She watches Ting all day, and I relieve her as soon as I get home from work. Mom goes to bed around nine p.m., then I stay awake with Ting for as long as I can, which is usually until two or three a.m. Mom sets the alarm for four a.m. so that, in the end, Ting is only unsupervised for an hour or two. Each morning, before I head out, I watch Ting while Mom takes a quick shower, then gathers all the food and water she'll need for herself for the day so that she doesn't have to leave the room. It's depressing, stressful, lonely work for Mom, and the last thing she needs so soon after Dad's death. But we have no other option.

Weeks go by, eventless. Ting doesn't have a single spell. Her skin becomes raw where the sensors are attached, and we have to take her to Bulger to have them repositioned. By then she has gone through seven rolls of pet wrap. I ask Dr. Belden if sometimes cats who have this condition get better on their own. "Not that I've seen," she says, which is her way of saying, "Never. No." Pessimistic that this waiting game will end anytime soon, we leave Bulger with half a dozen rolls of pet wrap.

As time passes, we start to doubt whether there was ever anything wrong with Ting in the first place—to wonder if, knee-deep in grief over Dad, we had simply *imagined* the worst: that we were on the brink of losing the only thing we had left except each other. In one of my crazier moments, I secretly Google "Munchausen syndrome by proxy" to see if it's applicable to pets. Rare, but not unheard of, my computer tells me.

As we're monitoring Ting, we're also monitoring each other—on the lookout for signs that the other is starting to lose it. I see a pile of unopened bills that has been sitting there for a week, and just before I say something about late fees, Mom mentions that she plans to make tomorrow "bill day." She hears me talking to myself in my room late at night, and when she asks me about it the next day, I tell her the truth: I was rerecording the outgoing message on my voicemail at work.

Throughout the monitoring process, we're in constant contact with Dr. Laste, who tells us this lack of cardiac events isn't unheard of, and encourages us to remain vigilant. Eventually, on a cloudy Wednesday in early October, it pays off: Ting passes out while I'm at work, Mom hits RECORD, then dials the 800 number to transmit the info.

The next day, Dr. Laste calls to tell us she got what she needed. She's ready to schedule the surgery.

If only Mom and I felt as ready.

CHAPTER FIFTEEN

Pacing

*A house isn't a home without the ineffable contentment of
a cat with its tail folded about its feet.*

—L. M. MONTGOMERY

As the day of Ting's surgery approaches, Mom and I
are wracked with guilt over what we're about to put her
through. Ting has never spent a night away from us, and
we're afraid she'll think we've abandoned her forever.
We're afraid she'll be terrified by all the strange people
who'll be touching her—all the strange sights, sounds, and
smells. We ask each other again and again whether we're
doing the right thing. Our research has shown us it's not a

surgery that always goes smoothly, and even when it does, there can be huge complications later. The lead can slip off the heart. Scar tissue can form around it, blocking the current, rendering it useless. And, of course, any surgery involving anesthesia has its risks.

Given how small Ting is, we can't imagine how someone—even someone as skilled as Dr. Laste, who is kind of a tiny person herself—will be nimble enough to do what needs to be done to her walnut-size heart. I try to calm myself by researching surgery performed on babies in utero, calculating that if heart surgery can be performed on an unborn child, it can surely be performed on a cat of similar size, especially when there's a lot more space to maneuver. Meanwhile, Mom has located information on a ferret who had a successful pacemaker implantation by a doctor at Tufts University's Cummings School of Veterinary Medicine. Ting is much bigger than a ferret, we rationalize.

Still, we keep second-guessing ourselves. The only thing we don't hesitate over is the cost, steep though it is. We believe animals have as much right to good health care as people do. And it's a good thing we feel that way, because between the surgery itself, the anesthesia, the pacemaker, the X-rays to make sure it's positioned properly, the pain medication and antibiotics after, and the stay in the hospital, we're looking at around $10,000. We're grateful we

have savings, and think of the families who couldn't afford this for their child, much less their cat.

The night before the surgery, we don't sleep. I think back to the night before Dad's bypass surgery more than a dozen years ago—to the special soap he had to shower with, the sleeping pill they prescribed for him. I think back to Dad's cardiothoracic surgeon, the aptly named Dr. Payne. I don't ask Mom if she's thinking of these things, too, but I'm pretty sure she is. Except for my four years in college— when, truth be told, I called her every day—we've lived pretty much the exact same life ever since I was born. We can usually guess what the other is thinking. We can start and finish each other's sentences. It used to drive Dad nuts.

On the morning of the surgery, before the sun is even up, Mom and I cajole Ting into her cat carrier and drive the hour to Angell, arriving at 7:30 a.m. The place is already bustling—businesspeople taking their dogs and cats for routine appointments before heading to work; nervous pet parents who brought their dog or cat, rabbit or parakeet, to Angell first thing, after a long, dark night of worry. I've taken the day off, but I'm wearing business clothes in the hope that, if I don't like how Ting is being treated and have to speak up, I'll at least be taken seriously. It's silly, really— the doctors at Angell are always respectful, and they treat their patients with so much care. But ever since losing Dad, I always dress for battle.

We're ushered into an exam room—a different one than the last time—where we take Ting out of her carrier and take turns kissing her on the forehead before handing her over to one of the nurses, telling her to be brave and that we'll be right there when she gets out. She's shaking. She knows where she is and that something bad is about to happen. I'm tempted to wrap her in my sweater and run, but the best thing I can do for her is relinquish.

We wait dutifully in the "cats" area, drinking too-strong tea from the vending machine, and alternating our trips to the ladies' room so that one of us is always there should a nurse or doctor come looking for us. We don't engage in conversation with any of the other cat people, because we don't want to have to explain that our cat is our entire world, and that, somewhere down the hall, someone is attaching an electrode to her heart—that normally we'd be sympathetic, but today their kitten's fleas, or infected paw, or runny nose are irrelevant to us. We don't engage in conversation with each other because at times like these, we can't be civil—we're just too tightly wound.

I have read that this surgery takes sixty to ninety minutes. Almost two hours have gone by. Every time the door to the surgery wing opens, I expect someone to come through it and give us devastating news, like they did with Dad. Finally, Dr. Laste comes out, and as she walks briskly across the lobby she flashes us a double thumbs-up and gives us a giant smile. I bite the inside of my bottom lip in an effort to keep from crying. When she gets to us, I hug her first, then Mom does.

She tells us all is well, but that it was touch and go for a while—that as she was trying to sew on the lead, Ting's heart rate dropped precipitously. However, Dr. Laste had anticipated this before the surgery even started, and had placed an external pacing wire through an artery in Ting's neck just in case a jump was needed before the permanent pacemaker was safely in place. We are thankful for Ting's cautious doctor. We're thankful, too, that she feels good about where she placed the pacemaker—just under the skin on Ting's left side (her "left flank," as they call it), far enough back so that it won't affect the use of her front legs, and far enough forward that she'll still be able to use her hind legs to jump. What's more, even though she's fourteen years old, her skin is thick enough that Dr. Laste didn't have to implant the pacemaker under muscle, which can lead to involuntary spasms, or, worse, in her stomach, which is sometimes the only option, and which, of course, can lead to all kinds of digestive issues.

Dr. Laste's description of the surgery is, by necessity, simplified for us. But here's what actually happened, according to Ting's medical records:

Left lateral thoracotomy performed at 6th intercostal space. Pericardium opened and four stay sutures of 4-0 nylon placed to create pericardial sling. Region of left ventricle located that did not have obvious coronary arteries present selected for pacemaker placement. Two interrupted sutures of 4-0 silk placed parallel to one another and used to secure pacemaker electrode in place. Electrode checked for function. Pericardium closed over electrode with 3-0 PDS in simple continuous pattern with 1 cm opening at ventral aspect. 3 cm incision in left dorsal flank. Blunt dissection ventral to incision to create pocket. Pacemaker wire passed through ventral 7th intercostal space and through subcutaneous tissue to left flank incision. Pacemaker attached to lead and secured in subcutaneous pocket with 2-0 nylon dermal interrupted suture. Lavage of thorax. Placement of 8 Fr chest tube. Thorax closed with circumcostal sutures of 0 Surgipro in interrupted pattern. Muscular layers (serratus ventralis, latissimus dorsi) closed in simple continuous pattern of 3-0 PDS. Subcutaneous closure with 3-0 PDS, simple continuous pattern. Skin closed with 3-0 nylon in Ford interlocking pattern. Incision over pacemaker closed with subcutaneous 3-0 PDS simple continuous. Skin closed with 3-0 nylon in Ford interlocking pattern. Chest tube secured with purse string and finger-trap of 2-0 nylon.

And all of this takes place in about eight pounds' worth of space.

Dr. Laste walks us back to the recovery room. Ting is laid out on a table on top of several blankets, a critical care nurse standing beside her. Her eyes are completely open, but she's still pretty out of it due to the anesthesia. Occasionally she tries to lift her head, but it's clear the effort depletes her. The fur has been shaved off one side of her neck, her chest, and her abdomen, and above her left front paw. A row of sloppy stitches pokes out from the gauze.

"I'm sorry they're not neater," says Dr. Laste. "We rushed to close so we could bring her out of sedation." Ting has a drainage tube in her chest, an IV in her front leg, and an oxygen mask on her face. I can't help but think of Dad—how he looked in his last hours.

We're shown back out to the waiting area and told we can see Ting again in a few hours, after the anesthesia has worn off and they've gotten her settled in her cage. We're not hungry, but we want to keep our strength up because we know these next few days will be tough. We're afraid to leave the hospital in case Ting takes a turn for the worse, so Mom goes to the front desk and asks the receptionist if they know of a place that delivers. They do, of course—even furnish us with a menu. Forty-five minutes later we're eating Caesar salad wraps and drinking fresh-squeezed lemonade.

I feel guilty enjoying a meal while Ting is all alone, and probably scared, and possibly in pain, even though they have a pain management specialist on staff who'll be monitoring her closely. I feel guilty about a lot of things lately—almost everything, really. It seems wrong to eat a sandwich when Dad doesn't get to. It seems wrong to take a Saturday-afternoon nap, wrong to drink hot chocolate (even just the instant kind), wrong to spend an hour reading the *Boston Sunday Globe*, wrong to play a game of Scrabble. In short, it seems wrong to do anything he'd have liked doing.

I know Mom feels it too, because there are things we just don't do anymore—and we don't discuss not doing them. Most noticeably, we avoid going to the Chinese restaurant where Dad took us every Friday night—the one in the nearby strip mall with the all-you-can-eat buffet; the one Dad used to call the Panda Palace, even though that wasn't its name; the one where the waitresses just waved us in because they knew which booth we'd sit at, and that we didn't need menus. I missed being a regular. I missed hanging out with my dad. I missed the predictable path his meal would take—hot and sour soup; chicken and broccoli over rice; a crab rangoon or egg roll if Mom wasn't looking (a pan-seared pot sticker if she was); a sparerib or two if he was in the mood to withstand a lecture from me on the intellectual similarities between pigs and canines.

I had started to process the fact that half my safety net had disappeared when Dad died, but I was still struggling with the small, subtle ways a death in the family changes things—how it alters daily routines and makes everything good fair game for guilt. My one comfort was that Dad didn't have to go through all of this drama with Ting. I'm not sure he could have hacked it; I wouldn't have wanted him to have to.

As the start of visiting hours approaches, the lobby begins to get full. Finally, a woman with a clipboard comes out and begins to read off names: Smokey, Peanut, Samson,

Chloé. After what seems like ages she calls Ting-Pei, and we're escorted back to see her, our heels clicking on the floor. They've situated her at the end of a row in an oxygen chamber—not because she needs constant oxygen, but because it's quieter and more out of the way. Thoughtful of them.

Still, Ting seems miserable. She's hiding under a thin white towel they've left with her for just that purpose (her pale-yellow one remains with us so that it doesn't get lost), because we've told them she's a burrower. When we unlatch the door the white towel starts to shake. I inch it back from her face so she can see it's just us, and when she does, she lets out a volume-ten yowl that makes the other families look up from their own pets.

The fur around Ting's eyes is slightly matted from the ointment they put in to keep them moist during surgery. It's all too familiar. Mom takes a tissue from her purse and starts to clean Ting's face, while I stroke the top of her head—the only part of her I'm certain won't be sore. After a couple of minutes Ting tries to stand up, but the IV in her front leg and the gauze that's wrapped around it makes it impossible to balance, and she rolls back onto her side, which is also thoroughly wrapped in gauze and thankfully doesn't look to be seeping.

According to her chart she's getting three different kinds of pain medication: Hydromorphone (a form of

morphine) through her IV, 15 milligrams of Gabapentin (used to relieve nerve pain) by mouth three times a day, and constant Fentanyl from a patch. We're confident she's as comfortable as she can possibly be, but we're pretty sure that's not too comfortable.

She tolerates us petting her for a while, but there's no purring, and we can tell she's exhausted. Mom tucks the towel around her and, as quietly as possible, I close the door and latch it. Soon she settles down and falls asleep. We stand there watching her until visiting hours end.

CHAPTER SIXTEEN

Homecoming Again

The cat does not offer services. The cat offers itself. Of course he wants care and shelter. You don't buy love for nothing.

—WILLIAM S. BURROUGHS

There's a lot more love in a house when there's a cat. Ting has to stay at Angell for almost a week, and the place is quiet and strange without her. And Dad is deader, somehow, when Ting's not around.

Mom and I go to visiting hours each day—me leaving work early to get there, Mom driving down from home. We come to know some of the other animals at Angell and what they're there for. There's a Great Dane around the corner from Ting who is undergoing chemo for lung cancer. The nurses have put a soft mat down on the floor of his closet-size cage, and when his people visit, they lie right down and curl up next to him. They only get up when the oncologist stops by to give them a progress report. The cancer sounds formidable, but they seem hopeful.

We become friends with an impeccably dressed woman named Pilar whose Cavalier King Charles Spaniel, Penelope, had spinal surgery around the same time Ting had her pacemaker implanted. Penelope's cage is below and just to the right of Ting's. Like us, Pilar never misses visiting hours. And, like us, her pet's recovery is going more slowly than expected. Penelope still can't use her back legs. Pilar is sturdy, like Hemingway's boat—for which she was or wasn't named (I never get the chance to ask)—and we know that, when she finally gets to take Penny home, she'll carry her upstairs if Penny can't get there under her own power. Still, we hope it doesn't come to that. For Penny's sake, and for Pilar's, we want to see Penny walk.

As the week goes on, we become increasingly concerned. Ting's not eating. She's not drinking. With little going in, nothing's coming out. We bring her her own food from home, but she shows absolutely no interest. The nurses try everything from tuna to Meow Mix, which they tell us is pretty much crack for cats. Ting turns her nose up at it. Though they haven't even mentioned it yet, we're afraid they're going to have to resort to a feeding tube. We don't know if it'd mean a tube down her nose or a tube in her side, and we're too afraid to ask. Either way, we want to avoid it. Our cat has been through enough.

Ting is losing weight by the day, and Mom and I agree that what she needs is to come home—to get back to familiar surroundings and her usual routine. To get back to her people. We talk with Dr. Laste, who says it's worth a try, and lets us sign her out. A usually silent passenger, Ting gives us an earful the entire ride back to New Hampshire—all along Storrow Drive, straight up 93, and onto bumpy Pond Street, where, just briefly, she's jostled into silence.

Her first days at home are a blur. Normally we pick her up without thinking—left hand under her chest, right hand supporting her back legs—and, in one smooth motion, tuck her body against ours. It was as natural for us as breathing. But now we're oddly tentative, afraid we're going to jostle the pacemaker somehow and hurt her. She senses our hesitance, and tenses when we approach.

Wanting to sleep next to her but afraid she might fall off the bed, we take turns sleeping on the floor beside her—positioned so that, if she tries to get up, one of us will know it. Each morning, she steps into her litter box and sits there, confused. After a few minutes, she paws at nothing—dainty habit—and stumbles out. She's not grooming herself at all, and grooming is the sign of a happy, healthy cat. Her fur is starting to get matted in places, so Mom and I tear up one of my old T-shirts, wet the strips slightly with lukewarm tap water, and take turns bathing her in long, languid strokes, just like her cat mother would have done, in the hope it'll somehow seem familiar.

When we hold a glass of water up to her, Ting laps a little bit, but she's still not eating. We keep dry food in her bowl at all times, just in case, but each morning we end up dumping it in the toilet and replacing it with fresh. I set Ting on our bathroom scale to try to gauge her weight, but she won't stay on it—won't stand still. I pick her up in my arms, step on the scale, and subtract a hundred pounds. It leaves me with just over six. She's lost almost two pounds.

Desperate, we call Dr. Belden for advice. She recommends we swaddle Ting in a towel and force-feed her canned cat food using a syringe—squirt it right down her throat, around the clock, every two hours. Mom goes to Bulger to get the syringe and some special high-nutrient cat food. When she gets home, we take turns trying to feed Ting, but it doesn't work any better than it sounds like it'll work. Even though she's weak, Ting fights us tooth and nail. The cat food gets in my hair and underneath my fingernails. Mom ends up wearing more of it than Ting ingests. But we keep trying. We set every alarm we have so that every two hours, something goes off.

Back when Ting first started wearing the heart monitor, we moved her kitty bed from its usual spot on top of Dad's armoire to the top of Mom's dresser, which was quite a bit lower. Because she's not yet strong enough to hop up and sleep in it, we decide to construct an elaborate tepee for her to rest in. I drag the clothes rack from the basement and splay it open beside the orange chair in Mom's room, draping it with a couple of towels. Mom tests each of the pillows on her bed, then sets the softest one on the floor of the tent. Gingerly I set Ting in. She stays and, minutes later, we hear her snoring. We check her more often than we should, to make sure she's still alive.

Ting-Pei has become a team effort, more than ever before. If Mom and I feel like squabbling in that very special way that mothers and daughters do, we have no choice but to bury the hatchet. We have a cat who needs us. If we want to take our grief out on each other, we can't; we need each other too much, and Ting needs us to work together.

We're desperate to help Ting get better, so we take to the Internet for ideas. We come across a *Scientific American* article by a professor at the UC Davis School of Veterinary Medicine who explains that cats purr at a frequency between 25 and 150 hertz, and that frequencies in this range have been shown to increase bone density and encourage healing—in the animal as well as the human. It sounds a little woo-woo to us, but we figure, what the hell, and make a chart on which we can track the ten five-minute "purring sessions" per day that we've assigned ourselves. We use a combination of kisses, brushes, scratches, and rubs to elicit the desired sound, and Ting is more than compliant. I catch myself wondering if this will help Mom's osteoporosis, too.

Because Ting hasn't been getting adequate nourishment, her incisions are slow to heal, so Dr. Belden advises us to leave the stitches in an extra week. That means more time in pet wrap—hot pink this time—though Ting clearly does not appreciate her mummified state. Somehow she manages to loosen her bandages enough that she literally walks right out of them. She does it again and again. We call Dr. Belden once more, and she suggests a onesie with the bottom part—the crotch with the snaps—cut off. Mom marches off to Walmart while I watch Ting, and comes back with package after package, because, really, what size onesie fits an eight-pound cat? Preemie? Newborn? Six-month-old? None of them, it turns out—especially when the cat views the outfit as the ultimate indignity.

As for me, I'm not unaware that I've become a thirty-six-year-old single woman who lives with her mom and dresses her cat in baby clothes. But I don't care. I've shimmied far enough up Maslow's hierarchy that it doesn't much matter what others think about me. All I want is for Ting to be well. She has seen me through 9/11, through a long and ill-conceived war, through the end and the start of a century, and through the loss of my dad. She has spanned three decades of my life, and she has been its constant.

But mostly I want her to be okay because I love her—because she is a sweet and wonderful creature who deserves a good, long life.

It's another week before Ting rounds the corner. During that time we keep doctors Laste and Belden up-to-date via e-mail, and even bring Ting to Bulger once because she's losing so much weight. Dr. Belden isn't there that day, but one of her colleagues prescribes an antinausea medication and, miraculously, it works. Finally, Ting eats some food on her own—just a little dry, but it's a great sign.

Mom and I debate whether to continue to force-feed her—whether it'll hijack her own efforts, or whether she needs it because the amount she's consuming on her own just isn't sufficient. Dr. Belden advises us to cut back on the force-feeding, but not to stop it altogether. We comply, and soon enough we can tell that Ting is almost back to her fighting weight. In fact, she gains enough energy to rip out the stitches that are holding the pacemaker in place. I hear the sound—like a zipper—during one of the rare moments we're not watching her, but can't get to her in time to stop her. Thankfully she has healed enough that the skin stays together.

Soon her fur grows back. She is her old self again, save for a pronounced bump near her ribs—like the face of a watch atop a tiny wrist. She is completely oblivious to it.

CHAPTER SEVENTEEN

Manuscript

The only thing a cat worries about is what's happening right now. As we tell the kittens, you can only wash one paw at a time.

—LLOYD ALEXANDER

We couldn't save my father, but we have saved his cat. It was a year of loss and almost loss, of sucker punch after sucker punch, of learning how best to love what's left. But we made it.

As it says in the Talmud, "Who saves one life saves the entire universe." It doesn't specify the kind of life, human or animal. We didn't save the universe by saving Ting, but to a great extent we saved *our* universe, because that's what she is to us. She has always been that to all of us—to me, to Mom, to Dad.

Three years passed, uneventful. Then, on a warm day in late September, part of me went numb—specifically, my left leg, followed the next day by my left arm, followed the day after that by the lower right side of my face, followed in quick succession by the right side of my tongue. At first I blamed it on the red grapes my mom had been giving me to take to work. Some particularly toxic pesticide, perhaps? Had she gotten them at the regular market instead of at Whole Foods? She assured me I was crazy—that, yes, she *had* gotten the grapes at the regular market, but that she, too, had eaten them and felt fine, and that she had washed them thoroughly prior to tucking them in my purse.

Explanation two involved Monks Blend tea, which a colleague had given me as a gift, and which I'd never tried before. It was excellent, strong, fancy black tea, with the subtlest hint of vanilla—but a quick Google search revealed that it also contained grenadine. Could I be allergic to grenadine? To be on the safe side, I switched back to my old reliable, Lipton.

A week went by. Still numb. Walking was becoming a challenge. A couple of times I nearly toppled over when bending to pick up Ting. While not ruling out the very real possibility that my mother or colleague had inadvertently poisoned me, I decided I'd better go to the doctor. Truth be told, I was more annoyed than worried. I was so unsteady that I'd had to stop wearing heels—and none of my pants were hemmed for flats.

Usually healthy as a horse, I didn't even have a primary care physician. I called the office of one who I'd gone to twenty years ago, and left a message asking if she'd see me. Her receptionist never called me back. After much nagging by Mom, I called to find out how late the local walk-in clinic was open, and on October 2, drove myself there after work.

ConvenientMD wasn't crowded that night. There were just two people ahead of me—a little boy with his arm in a cast, and an elderly man with a gauze-covered chin. I scanned my iPhone for media hits, for mentions of my publishing company's books. I checked the next day's weather report. I deleted some spam from my in-box. Whatever was going on with me, I wanted to fix it and get on with my life.

When my name was called, I walked into the exam room at my normal speed, but whacked my shoulder on the doorjamb. No one saw it, so I just pretended like nothing had happened. The physician's assistant listened intently as I rattled off my symptoms. She took my temperature (normal) and blood pressure (nice and low). She had me squeeze her hands and touch each of my fingers to my thumb. She had me close my eyes and raise my arms above my head. Everything she asked me to do, I did with ease. I appeared to be neurologically intact. She went out and talked with the doctor, came back, and gave me an EKG. I thought of Dad and I thought of Ting as she pressed the electrodes onto my skin.

Five minutes later, the doctor came in.

"Your EKG looks great," she said.

She repeated a bunch of the tests her assistant had done, then asked if I could be drunk or pregnant.

"Neither, unfortunately," I said. "Though I can see how one could lead to the other."

She said I needed blood work and an MRI, but that they'd have to send the blood to a lab, and that they couldn't do the MRI there. She wanted me to go to an emergency room, and said she'd call ahead to fill them in. I thought it was odd—I didn't feel *that* bad—but said okay, so long as it wasn't the hospital where my dad had died.

She went out and came back ten minutes later. She had called ahead to Holy Family, a small hospital close to my house, and spoken with a Dr. Cohen, who'd be expecting me. Sounded like a perfect fit for a half-and-half girl like me: Catholic hospital, Jewish doctor. As the physician's assistant walked me out, she asked me if I wanted a wheelchair. I pretended like I hadn't heard her.

I got lost on the way to the hospital, so deep in thought that I drove right past the street it was on. Having discarded my grape and tea theories, which the ConvenientMD doc had pooh-poohed, I had narrowed it down to four possibilities: stroke, brain tumor, multiple sclerosis, and vitamin B deficiency. I was certainly rooting for the latter.

When I finally found my way to the hospital, the registration nurse who checked me in asked if I wanted a wheelchair after watching me make my way toward a bench in the lobby. The ER nurse who called me in minutes later did the same thing as I walked through the ER's bright blue double doors. Why was everyone offering me a wheelchair? I knew I wasn't walking quite right, but I didn't think it was obvious. And to an untrained eye, perhaps it wasn't. No one at work had noticed anything. These were medical professionals, though—and their thoughtfulness was scaring me.

Two hours passed before Dr. Cohen came to see me. I wasn't happy to be kept waiting, but I reasoned that there were probably people much sicker than I in the ER that night. What's more, I figured I could rule out stroke; if the doctor at ConvenientMD had had the least suspicion of that, I'm certain the ER doctor would have gotten to me sooner, because every minute counts with stroke.

Dr. Cohen repeated the neurological exams that had been done twice at the walk-in clinic and asked me similar questions. Then he glanced at the EKG printout, which I excavated from my purse with no small amount of difficulty because the fingers on my left hand were so numb. He saw me fumbling, and asked how long they'd been like that.

"Just a few days," I said. "I keep thinking I'll just get better. Honestly, I'm never sick. I'm that person who doesn't get the flu when the rest of the office has it. I don't even have a primary care physician."

"You should really get one," he said. And then, seeing the concerned look on my face, "Everyone should. It's how the system works."

"How nice for the system," I said. "So, blood work and MRI?" It was, after all, the reason I'd been sent here—and it was closing in on eleven p.m.

"It's too late for that," he told me. "The lab has closed, and we only do MRIs after hours when there's risk to life or limb."

"So I'm not in imminent danger?" I asked. "You're sure it's not a stroke?"

"It's not a stroke, but you do need to see a neurologist to figure out what's going on."

"Okay," I said. "I'll Google one." Google—my answer for everything.

"Actually," he said, "I'll make a call for you. I know a good one."

A few minutes later he came back with a page from his prescription pad. On it, a phone number and the name Dr. Richard Finkelman.

"I spoke with Dr. Finkelman," the ER doctor told me. "He said to call his office first thing tomorrow; he'll leave word with his receptionist to fit you right in."

I didn't know whether to be pleased or alarmed that an ER doc was willing to call a neurologist at home at eleven p.m., and that a neurologist was willing to squeeze me in the following day, but decided I'd sleep much better that night if I went with "pleased." I thanked the doctor and walked down the ER hallway and out to the lobby, concentrating with every step so that no one could tell there was anything wrong with me.

When I called the next morning, Dr. Finkelman's receptionist said to come in at eleven a.m., and they'd fit me in somehow. I e-mailed my boss to tell him I'd be late to work that day, but would be in as soon as I could. Dr. Finkelman's office was a few towns away, in Haverhill, an old mill town not unlike the one in which my father had died.

I found the building easily enough, parked, entered through the main lobby, and took the elevator to the fourth floor. The waiting room was crowded—lots of people with walkers, canes, and wheelchairs. I found it unsettling, but focused on the forms the receptionist had told me to fill out. They didn't take long. I wasn't on any medication, had never been diagnosed with any medical condition other than Raynaud's, and the only surgery I'd ever had was to remove my wisdom teeth.

About a half-hour later, the receptionist called my name and I was ushered in. I liked Dr. Finkelman instantly. We chatted about our families as he ran me through the same silly tests I'd undergone three times the night before. He spent a long time looking at my eyes with a little light that made them water.

"Sorry," he said. "Just trying to visualize your optic nerves. They look fine. In fact, everything looks fine. But let's do blood work and an MRI."

"With or without gadolinium?" I asked, trying to get a feel for what he was looking for. I'd been Googling most of that morning. I knew dye would be needed to rule things in or out.

"With contrast," he said. "Why do you ask?"

"Just trying to figure out what you think is wrong with me."

"What do *you* think is wrong with you?" he asked. I would learn later that he had dual degrees in neurology and psychiatry.

I listed my contenders: "MS, brain tumor, or maybe just a vitamin B12 deficiency."

"How'd you come up with those?" he asked.

I explained that the company I worked for had published a memoir by a woman with MS, and that some of my symptoms sounded like hers—and that I knew that's why he was trying to get a look at my optic nerves; that I didn't know much about brain tumors, but that given my symptoms they seemed plausible and I'd like to rule them out; that I ate a pretty much vegetarian diet, so my B12 level could very well be low.

Dr. Finkelman seemed amused.

"Well," he said, "we'll know more after you go downstairs." Turns out they had a lab and an MRI machine on the first floor. I'd walked right by them on my way to the elevator.

Having blood drawn had never bothered me, so long as they didn't have to fish for a vein. In fact, I was so unfazed by it that I'd always thought it a shame I fell short of the 110 pounds you're required to weigh to donate blood.

"Your veins are really small," the phlebotomist said.

"Sorry," I said. "I actually had a couple bottles of water on the way here this morning. I wanted to plump them up for you."

"It's no problem," she said. "We'll find one."

After a couple of tourniquet ties and several minutes of hunting with the pads of her fingertips—reading Braille along my forearms—she located one that looked good to her.

"Let's try this one here," she said, pointing to an almost invisible vein on the inside of my right elbow. She proceeded to hit it on the first try.

Several vials later, I was ushered into the MRI room and told to lie down on the table that would slide me into the machine. I'd purposely worn clothes that didn't have snaps or zippers so that I wouldn't have to change into a hospital gown, and I'd slipped my little silver earrings into my purse. The nurse gave me a blanket, and proceeded to ask me a bunch of questions, including whether I was claustrophobic and whether I had a pacemaker.

"Confined spaces don't bother me," I said. "And I don't have a pacemaker, but my cat does."

"I didn't know they made pacemakers for cats," she said.

"They don't," I told her. "It's a human one."

She seemed only mildly impressed, and handed me some earplugs.

"This will be a little loud," she said, "but should only take forty minutes."

"When do you give me the contrast?" I asked.

"Oh," she said, "your insurance declined it. We're going to do it without the gad."

"Does Dr. Finkelman know that?" I asked.

She assured me that he did. I considered protesting, but figured if he wasn't concerned, I shouldn't be either. And, truth be told, I felt like I'd gotten lucky in the lab a few minutes prior, and didn't want to tempt fate with another stick.

"Do you want to listen to music while you're in there?" she asked.

"Do you get NPR?"

"What's NPR?"

"National Public Radio," I said. "*Fresh Air? On Point? Diane Rehm?*" I could tell none of them were ringing a bell.

"Like, New Hampshire Public Radio," I said, still searching for common ground. "*The Exchange? Word of Mouth?*" The local shows weren't any more familiar to her than the nationals.

"Never mind," I said, "it's not important. I'll be fine."

And with that, I popped in the earplugs and reclined on the MRI table. The nurse immobilized my head with foam cushions, pushed a button, and in I went.

The MRI machine was indeed really loud—lots of clanking, and whirring, and an odd kind of metallic purring. I thought of Ting, whose purr was soft and comforting, and only shared with a select few. I told myself that if there was something really wrong with me, at least Mom would be there to take care of her. Who would take care of Mom, I didn't know.

I tried not to let my thoughts turn dark. I told myself that this was probably just a lot of fuss over nothing—that I probably just needed to eat a little meat once in a while, to get enough B12.

From time to time, the nurse used the intercom to ask me how I was doing. But then, about twenty minutes into the procedure, the machine stopped purring and she came into the room.

"Guess what? We were able to get your insurance to okay the contrast after all," she said, as she rolled up my right sleeve to look for a vein.

"I had blood drawn from there a little while ago," I said from inside the machine. "Maybe try the other arm?" My head was still immobilized.

She rolled up my left sleeve, then turned her attention to the back of my left hand, then the back of my right hand, then back to my right arm.

"There's a vein beside the one they just used to draw blood," she said. "Let's try that." I smelled the alcohol as she swabbed my arm, but couldn't see what she was doing, which bothered me.

"Okay, deep breath," she said, as the needle pierced my skin. And a second later, "Damn—no return. I missed it."

"Don't fish," I said. "Take it out and try again."

"It's out," she said. "Sorry, that vein blew. Let's look at the left arm again."

She put a tourniquet on my left arm, slapped it a bit to try to raise the vein, and told me to pump my fist. "No," she said. "That's not going to work."

"Try one of my hands," I said, from inside the tube.

She picked up my right hand and examined it again.

"Okay, there's one here, but it's not great. Let's try it."

Alcohol again, and, once again, a miss.

"I'm sorry," she said. "I don't like hurting people. I'm usually good at this."

I could tell she was getting flustered.

"I see one in your wrist that's not great, but we'll try it," she said.

"The wrist ones hurt," I responded. "Don't. Maybe we should just do the rest without contrast."

"We *have* to find a vein," she said. Her voice had gone flat—all business. "You *need* this MRI with contrast."

It was then that I knew I was in trouble—that they'd seen something bad on the MRI; that a doctor had called my insurance company and insisted on the gad; that whatever he'd told them had made them cave.

"Okay," I said. "Do what you need to do."

"I'll try your right hand again," she said. And this time, somehow, she got it. Within seconds, I could taste the gadolinium in the back of my throat. And just as quickly, it was gone.

Twenty minutes later the MRI was done and I was on my way home to do a quick conference call before heading into the office. I was craving any distraction I could muster, needing the normality of work.

I called my mom to tell her what had transpired, and she told me I may have misinterpreted what the MRI nurse had said, and not to jump to conclusions. As a veteran of my father's medical odyssey and, before that, my grandmother's, I did my best to take her advice to heart. But things still felt ominous.

Fall was in the air but the sun was strong, and something about it reminded me of 9/11—how I'd driven home beneath a bright blue sky an hour after the buildings fell, and with them thousands of people who'd started their day thinking everything would be normal.

As I turned onto my street, my cell phone rang.

"Lissa, it's Danielle in Dr. Finkelman's office. Can you come in tomorrow morning to discuss your MRI results?"

"You have them already?" I asked, afraid I knew why the radiologist had rushed them.

"They're pretty prompt here," Danielle said.

"Umm, yes, okay. Tomorrow. But I could also come back this afternoon. It would save me a long night of worrying." Silence on her end, and then from me: "I'm pretty sure they found something."

"Let me talk with Dr. Finkelman and call you back," she said.

I went inside and updated my mom. This time she agreed that it didn't sound good. I checked the clock: almost two p.m.—time for my weekly call with our sales reps. Mom brought Ting downstairs so that she wouldn't meow in the background. I dialed in on Mom's landline and put my cell on vibrate. Halfway through the conference call, my cell started to buzz. I went out in the hall and answered.

"Lissa, it's Danielle. Can you come back now?"

This time I took Mom with me for support. We weren't in the waiting room for more than a half-hour when Dr. Finkelman came to the door himself and motioned me in. Mom and I had already agreed that I'd go in alone. Before I was even seated he said, "Well, you nailed it. You have MS."

For most of my adult life, those initials had been an abbreviation for "manuscript." Now, in the blink of an eye, they would forever stand for an incurable, demyelinating disease in which areas of scar tissue—scleroses—would periodically form on my brain. My *brain*. That is, if I had the good kind of MS.

"Relapsing-remitting?" I asked him.

"Yes," he said. And, anticipating my next question, "We can tell because some of the lesions are old—resolved on their own—and some of them are active. That's why we needed the contrast. The new ones kind of glow."

"Lesions, plural?" I asked.

"Yes," he said. "There are ten of them. There's a rather large active one on the right side of your brain. That's why your left side is numb."

With that, he turned his monitor around so I could see the scans.

"To be honest, it's big enough that I'm surprised you're walking."

That did it.

"Do you mind if I bring my mom in?" I asked. "She's right outside, and she's worried."

And she was outside, and she *was* worried—but by this point, so was I.

I went out and got her, waited until she sat down, and spat out "It's MS."

Mom looked at Dr. Finkelman and nodded. "Better than a brain tumor," she said.

"Absolutely," said Dr. Finkelman. "Actually, it's a great time to have MS."

Coming from anyone else, the statement would have been ridiculous. But the way he said it showed he knew how silly it sounded, even though it was unequivocally true. He then went on to say there were excellent medications for it—several of them, in fact—and that we'd figure out which one was best for me. He also said it was likely that they'd find a cure for it in my lifetime. But first, we needed to stop the flare that I was having. This was usually done by administering three one-hour infusions of a steroid called Solu-Medrol—a thousand milligrams, given on consecutive days. But because I was small, he wanted me to do three days of just five hundred milligrams each.

"Okay," I said, anxious to take action. "Starting first thing tomorrow?"

"I'd like you to start today," he said. "I can write you a note for work."

"Oh, no need; they take me at my word. Besides, I never take my sick days."

"Infusion it is, then," Dr. Finkelman said.

Most hospitals have infusion centers for this kind of thing, but by then it was almost five p.m., so the emergency room would be the only option. Dr. Finkelman informed me that, although his office looked unassuming, he was actually the head of neurology at nearby Merrimack Valley Hospital. He would call and tell them to expect me.

It was there that I had my fifth and sixth needle sticks of the day—with six being my ticket to Solu-Medrol-ville and, eventually, remission.

Once I got through my first MS flare, the enormity of it started to sink in.

MS doesn't mean a shorter life span, but it does mean possible blindness (usually temporary, usually one eye at a time) and potentially the loss of mobility (a third of people with MS are unable to walk, and some of the two-thirds who can need an assistive device like a cane or a walker). I firmly believe I'll be part of the two-thirds, and that I'll still be walking on my own when I'm eighty. I firmly believe I'll be lucky.

In fact, I believe I'm already lucky. To go from symptoms, to neurologist appointment, to MRI, to diagnosis in less than twenty-four hours is fortunate indeed. MS is tricky. It takes some people months, even years, to get an accurate diagnosis. It can be easily dismissed as a pinched nerve or fibromyalgia, and there are lots of MS mimics like lupus, Lyme disease, and stroke. And some people have to undergo a painful spinal tap to get their MS diagnosis. All I had to do was lie still in a tube for a bit.

I'm also lucky that I found Dr. Finkelman, who was up on all the latest medications, and quick to rule out ones that could have serious side effects (like liver damage, miscarriage, or brain infection) or lesser ones that would be especially upsetting to a woman my age (like hair loss).

He started me on Copaxone (official name, glatiramer acetate), a daily subcutaneous injection that lessens the MS relapse rate by 34 percent, though no one seems to be certain how. Dr. Finkelman also helped to arrange for a nurse named Annie to come to my house to show me how to administer the shots using a pen-like device called an Autoject.

The injections are honestly no big deal, and I say that as someone without a lot of fat to stab. I just turn the dial to four (the shortest needle depth), aim, and fire. If you were to watch my face when I press the button, you wouldn't see my expression change. If you watched my body, you wouldn't see me flinch. Some people compare it to a bee sting, but it's honestly nowhere near that bad. I do develop a welt after each injection—kind of like what you get after a mosquito bite, but bigger. It's gone, however, within a day or two, and supposedly after a few months of being on Copaxone, you pretty much stop getting the welts altogether. Even if I don't, they're a small price to pay for 45 percent fewer lesions.

Dr. Finkelman also had a knack for anticipating my concerns and questions—and amusing me in the process. For example, when he told me the largest lesion was "tumefactive," he was quick to say "Bad name, that. It has nothing to do with a tumor. It just means it's big."

When he asked me my ethnic background and whether I had any family history of MS, he followed with "Don't worry. Doesn't mean your kid will have it. There's a slight genetic predisposition, but environment also plays a role. People in cold states get it more often, and people of Northern European descent, especially the Irish."

"Not much I can do about that," I said. "Mom's maiden name is McKittrick."

"Be more Jewish," Dr. Finkelman quipped.

Despite how good Dr. Finkelman was to me and my complete trust in his abilities, all of my friends told me I should try to find a neurologist in Boston as well. My bluntest friend, Karen, said it best: "People fly from all over the world to avail themselves of the doctors who practice at Boston hospitals. You'd be an idiot not to. Go to Brigham and Women's; they have a whole MS Center, complete with an infusion room. Try to get in to see Dr. Howard Weiner. He's Ann Romney's doctor—and you know she goes to the best."

Sometimes luck is having friends who, when the chips are down, do your crazy medical Googling for you.

I figured getting an appointment with a VIP doc like Weiner would be next to impossible, so I e-mailed my colleague Merloyd for advice, recalling that she had some connections to people at Boston hospitals, having edited health books by such luminaries as breast cancer surgeon Dr. Susan Love (the first woman surgeon on the staff of Boston's Beth Israel Hospital) and pediatrician Dr. T. Berry Brazelton (who established the Touchpoints Center at Boston Children's Hospital). If she didn't know anyone at Brigham, no doubt she'd know someone who did. I was determined to network my way to good health.

Merloyd got right back to me to say she did know someone at Brigham, and that, actually, I did too. A decade ago I'd handled the publicity for a book she had edited, *Human Trials* by Susan Quinn. It was about a wonderful doctor at Brigham who was trying to find a cure for MS—Howard Weiner. She'd try to help me get in to see him.

As soon as she said it I recalled the book, of course, and before I could even finish a thank-you e-mail, she had e-mailed the author, explaining my situation and cc'ing me. Within ten minutes, I had a reply from the author saying she'd written to Dr. Weiner on my behalf. And within a half-hour, she forwarded his reply. He'd cc'd his office manager, Marilyn, asking her to schedule me when I called. I was in, and, again, I was lucky.

Merloyd wasn't the only colleague I told about my diagnosis. In fact, I told most of them—especially the ones I had worked with for years, including my boss. I didn't want the added stress of trying to cover up my illness, and I'm not, by nature, a person who likes to hide things. Besides, these people were my friends; I'd worked with many of them for over a decade.

They were all unfailingly supportive when I told them. One of the women in my department left flowers on my desk; the other left a brownie from my favorite bakery down the street. Both of them told me to just let them know if I needed any help, personal or professional. My counterpart in our marketing department gave me the name of an ophthalmologist his wife once saw for optic neuritis, just in case I ever needed it. A member of his team told me her dad and stepmom both had MS, and gave me a book about it that she'd been saving for them. She also told me they were doing really well—still walking unassisted, many years post-diagnosis—and her dad was on Copaxone, which he found to be effective and exceedingly tolerable.

To this day, I remain bolstered by stories of MSers who are doing well. And I'm amazed by the number of people who know someone who has MS, even though, according to the data I've seen, only one in 400,000 Americans have it. Only one in every 1,000 of those people have the tumefactive kind that I have, which means I should either play the lottery or definitely *not* play the lottery. When I told my friend Beth that I'm one of only 400 people in the United States that has tumefactive MS, without missing a beat she said, "Well, Lissa, we always knew you were special." She laughed when she said it, of course—and I did, too. She's an only child, like me—and we always think we're special.

I told other friends, too. My writer friend Annie mentioned a buddy of hers whom she refers to as "my friend who has MS who I always forget has MS." That's what I want to be. I don't want people to think of me as a sick person, because I don't really think of myself that way. Not yet, at least. I'm not naive; I know this is a progressive disease. But I'm optimistic, and not afraid. I have MS, but it doesn't have me. It's clichéd, of course. But it's accurate.

Right now, unless you're staring at my MRI scans and the parts of my brain that look like they're covered in snow, my MS is an "invisible disease." That's both a blessing and a curse. It means no pity from friends or strangers, which is awfully nice, but sometimes it also means little help or understanding. I wish the people who know me best could have MS for five minutes each, preferably during the flare stage (when people with MS are at their worst), just so they'd know what it's like to try to walk across the room gracefully when you feel like you're balanced on a skateboard that's balanced on a boat—a boat that's spinning on a lazy Susan—with one-gallon water jugs strapped to your calves. People have asked me what having MS is like, and this is one way to describe it.

It's like trying to walk along a beach where the uneven sand exhausts you, or across a field that's covered in a foot of pristine snow—except, of course, you're on asphalt, or the carpet in your own home. It's like trying to walk from the bar to the ladies' room after having one too many glasses of Shiraz, your balance off, your limbs heavy and unpredictable, and every move requiring the utmost concentration, just so you're not that girl who face-plants in the bar or, God help you, "that poor girl with MS"—the one who should know better than to wear heels . . . who does, in fact, know better, but isn't quite ready to give them up. Suffice it to say I don't drink, though; my body feels drunk enough. Speaking of which, even stone-cold sober I'd fail a field sobriety test these days. People with MS have trouble walking heel to toe, or balancing on one leg. So here's hoping I don't ever get pulled over, and that, if I do, the cop is really understanding.

Despite all the downsides of MS, there's something about the disease—any disease, maybe—that makes a person more attuned to how others are struggling. I see a man with a pronounced limp navigate a loosely cobblestoned sidewalk, and I know how much stamina and body awareness it requires to do something most people totally take for granted. I think, "My God, he's amazing"—that someone should applaud, or that tomorrow's *Boston Globe* should carry the headline "Pedestrian with Gait Issue Conquers Farnsworth Street."

When I see people pull into a handicapped parking spot, I no longer think "They better really need it." I *assume* they really need it. Sometimes I watch to see if they also need help. I'd like to think that, if they did, I'd try to help. If they waved me off, I'd say, "It's okay; I get it. I have MS." I'd like to think that would do it—that they'd let me help them out. This club we're in: It's crappy, and none of us signed up. But everyone in it speaks the same language, and we have each other's back.

More than anything, I don't want my MS to become *me*—to become an excuse to be selfish or self-involved.

I'll never forget the man at the Brigham and Women's MS Center who so gallantly struggled to hold the elevator door for me the first day I went to see Dr. Weiner in his second-floor office, almost knocking his walker over in the process, and the smile we exchanged when we both reached out to press "2." Or my sales rep friend, the first person in our New York office whom I told about my diagnosis, who did a double take and said, "You're kidding. Me too." Turns out he's had MS the whole time I've known him—more than fourteen years. Or the man I met on the Acela coming back from a business trip, who somewhere around Providence mentioned in passing that he had MS—literally *in passing*, because he was on his way to the café car to get us peanut M&Ms, even though if you have MS, walking on a moving train is harder than getting into Harvard.

How many other people with a chronic illness have I always just assumed were healthy? How many could have used a door held open for them, or some peanut M&Ms that they didn't have to go and get themselves, or a word or two of encouragement, like I got from my sales rep friend, who listened intently as I described my wobbly walking, and e-mailed me the next day with a simple *Teeter on!*

There's a certain camaraderie among people with MS—an "us against it" mentality. That's why I signed up for the MS Center's CLIMB study (Comprehensive Longitudinal Investigation of Multiple Sclerosis at Brigham and Women's Hospital), in the hope that, by charting the progression of my disease, some knowledge will be gained for the benefit of us all. A couple thousand others have signed up to do the same thing.

So there are at least two thousand people in the Boston area who have MS. Why am I one of them? Rather than think "Why me?" I prefer to think "Why not me?" Why not someone who is otherwise healthy? Why not someone who has people who care about her—people who will, if necessary, *take* care of her? Why not someone who has good insurance and can afford this disease (MS tests, infusions, and medications aren't cheap—and the MRIs cost an arm and a leg, especially when they include your spine)? Why not someone who is smart enough to understand the things her doctors tell her, and to do a bit of her own research besides? Why not someone who took years of dance lessons—whose balance is good, and whose body naturally compensates for its own weaknesses? Why not someone who thinks of her MS in metaphors involving beaches and wine and fields of snow—someone whose idea of a great

Friday night is a good book to read and a cat who'll use her ankle as a pillow while she reads it? Why not someone who won't miss hiking, or skiing, or going for a run, because she's not someone who ever did those things?

Genetic predisposition aside, I believe MS is the disease I was born to have. I'm okay, and I'm okay with having it. What Dad had was scarier, and he never once wallowed, and he never gave up. What Ting had was scarier, and she never once bit us.

So far I haven't bitten anyone either.

CHAPTER EIGHTEEN
My Father's Daughter

*Kind old ladies assure us that cats are often the best
judges of character. A cat will always go to a good man,
they say.*

—VIRGINIA WOOLF

In my favorite pictures of my father, he has his arms around
me. In the first one, taken when I was three or four, he has
picked me up and we're cheek to cheek, bare trees in the
background, sunny enough for us to be squinting and warm
enough that sweaters sufficed. It was fall on Fire Island, and
that's all that I remember. That, and being happy.

In the second one, I'm older—nine or ten. We're in Nags Head, North Carolina, and the ocean is behind us. We're holding onto a kite for dear life. He's tan and looks athletic. His left arm is draped around my shoulders. As for me, I look protected. I *was* protected, always.

My father and I were very much alike—more alike in temperament than my mother and I. She preferred adventure, while he and I liked to stay home. She craved novelty, while he and I liked routine. Though a very bright woman, her life isn't in her head the way it is for me, and was for Dad. She needed to do things to be content. Dad and I just needed to think about doing them.

Unlike me, my father had a less than idyllic childhood. Sure, there was stickball in the streets, and aunts and uncles and cousins for Shabbat, and the roar of Yankee Stadium through open windows on warm summer nights. But his father was emotionally distant, and his mother, whom he adored, died when he was just thirteen. His father remarried a woman with children of her own. She wanted nothing to do with my dad, and he was left to his own devices at an age when he still needed tenderness and guidance. He floundered for several years—went off to college too young (a mere sixteen), then went straight to law school, dropped out and joined the navy, married a woman he barely knew, and got divorced from her soon after. They were tough years for him.

But my father was resilient. He began a successful career in retail, met and eventually married my mom, had a child (me), and became an involved and nurturing father who made it his life's mission to expose me to everything he knew, be it comic books or coins, lightning bugs or baseball cards, tropical fish or gefilte fish. I could never get behind the latter, but everything else became part of who I am. What I took away from him most—in addition, of course, to his love of animals—was his optimism and his ability to notice and appreciate kindness, as well as his respect for those who practiced it. My father was a very verbal man; he loved to tell stories. Not all of them had happy endings, but all of them had heroes. And he was, and always will be, mine.

While there are so many things I love about Ting, things that are unique to her, I'll admit that, like my father, I'm a sucker for cats in general. Dogs are nice, but their love is given freely. With cats you have to earn it, and I'm a girl who likes a challenge. A cat's love isn't earned easily, though. Food won't do it; neither will catnip. Petting and scratching help, but are wholly insufficient if not accompanied by constancy, consistency, and permanence. A cat knows when she'll always have you, and that's when she'll let you truly know her.

I like cats so much that I like phrases about them—even ones that don't really make sense: the cat's pajamas, cat got your tongue, the cat's meow, let the cat out of the bag. I like songs with cats in them, especially "Cat's in the Cradle," which topped the Billboard charts when I was two, Johnny Cash's "Mean Eyed Cat," and, for obvious reasons, The Cure's "All Cats Are Grey." I collect little books about kittens and cats, miniature volumes of sayings with line art. The sayings are trite, the line drawings bad—yet they hold a place of esteem on my mantel, buttressed by cat-shaped bookends. I can't explain it, really. Can't justify the cat-covered teacups with the matching dish towels, the bees-wax crouching-cat candle, the cat-shaped (God help me) oven mitts, or the cat-shaped cupcake tray. All I can say in my defense is that I. Love. Cats.

I love cats for their cat-like ways: for the paw draped dramatically over their eyes while they nap their way toward late afternoon. For their ability to become a ball— one that nestles and nuzzles and snores. For their Super-man stretches and their head butts to claim you. For how startled they look when they sneeze. For the carpet they claw while wiggling their ass, and the way they twitch while sleep-stalking a sparrow. For their teasey bites and their testy bites, and their incessant need to knead you. For the way that, once you've gained their trust, they'll literally walk all over you in an effort to get to your face to kiss you.

While I've never met a cat I didn't like, Ting-Pei is obviously special. She's our good luck cat, and I've learned a lot from her. But it was my father who taught me that, if we'd

all just spend a little more time looking for our good lucks, we'd see that they surround us. Ting is my daily reminder to look.

Dad was lucky to have Ting to make his last years happy. Ting was lucky to have skilled doctors who cared about her—skilled doctors who cared about us. Mom and I were lucky to have her to focus on during the worst of our grief, and she was lucky to have us to advocate for her and nurse her back to health. I'm lucky for my forty-one years without MS, a disease that strikes many in their twenties and thirties. And, when the time came, I was lucky to get a quick and accurate diagnosis.

Now I'm lucky to have Ting to cheer me up when my MS flares, lucky to have her beside me at this moment. But most of all, we're just lucky that a cat like her exists—that she came into our life and made our life her own.

Epilogue

Arise from sleep, old cat,
And with great yawns and stretchings . . .
Amble out for love

—KOBAYASHI ISSA

Multiple sclerosis translates to "many scars," and I suppose we all have them. Most of mine are literal now, black holes forming in my brain. But black holes give rise to galaxies, and I'm open to what this disease has to teach me. Always my father's daughter, I remain the hopeful Lissa Warren.

Ask how I am and I'll say "Good"—or, maybe, "Could be worse." Could be worse, have been worse, will be worse; all of them would be accurate. Close friends sometimes get

"Have been worse," with a bit of explanation. But "Will be worse" I save for Ting, who's tough enough to take it—who doesn't dwell on what's ahead because, today, there's sun to bask in.

If you were to ask me what I like best about MS—which, let it be known, no one ever asks me—I would say it's how the disease forces you to depend on others. Some people go weeks or months without a reminder of how much they're loved. I get those reminders daily: every time my mom opens a jar for me because my hands aren't very useful, every time a friend stands in line at Starbucks to get us tea while I sit at the table and wait. Of course the dependence is also what I like least about MS, and what I fear the most. But there you have it—life in all its messy glory. At least I'm alive to live it.

MS isn't cancer. It's not something you battle or something you fight. To use another military metaphor, MS isn't a war you win. It's something to which you acclimate, something you assimilate. They'll cure it in my lifetime, or they won't. If they don't, perhaps through new therapies or new medications, or both, they'll at least figure out a way to repair the damage done by MS lesions.

The first time I met him, I asked Dr. Weiner what I could do to improve my chances of living well with this disease. He told me to take my meds and keep a positive attitude. Done and done. Meanwhile, he's identifying genes associated with MS, while elsewhere on the Brigham and Women's campus, in a building I've probably passed a dozen times, another doctor bathes stem cells in acid, turning them embryonic. Hope.

Since my diagnosis, Mom has read eight books about MS. On the whole, she's doing pretty well. To be there for me, she stays closer to home now, busying herself around the house. She meets cousin Sonya for lunch and a movie. She bought herself an iPad and taught herself to use it. Some days she takes photos of Ting and sends them to me at work. When I travel for my job—which, thankfully, I'm still able to do—we keep in touch via Facetime. Same when she travels to upstate New York to see her best friend from high school, also named Donna. And she tries new recipes, like shrimp and risotto with asparagus (delicious) and cauliflower mashed potatoes (not). On Friday nights, I almost always get takeout from a nearby Mexican place that opened shortly after Dad died, to give Mom a break from cooking. We split an order of chicken fajitas and indulge in chips and salsa. Like the rest of the world, we got hooked on *Downton Abbey*, and subsequently found our way to other British PBS series, including *Mr. Selfridge*, which Mom really likes, because she worked in retail.

We bird-watch. We grow basil. We undercook brownies on purpose and use soup spoons to eat them hot. We appreciate the beautiful ordinary that is our lives. When we make tea for each other and set down the cups, it's Lissa on the left (because both words start with "L") and Mom on the right (because Mom's always right). We laugh when the nurse at the infusion center holds my IV in place with pet wrap.

I often marvel that Mom hasn't crumbled, and I've come to realize one reason she's so strong is that my father loved her so much, for so long. When a man gets such a kick out of you—spends forty years just being happy being with you—I guess it gives you the ability to get through anything. Even the loss of him. Even watching the daughter you taught to walk struggle to do so as an adult.

Ting is nineteen now, and a very happy cat. She's become quite vocal in her old age, and it seems to be particularly important to her that we know exactly where she is at all times. Consequently, she has developed the habit of announcing herself whenever she enters a room, or even just switches napping spots. So keeping tabs on her is fairly easy.

We spend our days trying to make things extra nice for her, whether it's switching on the lamp above her kitty bed when it's cloudy to make up for the absent sun, or leaving Dad's robe in the rocking chair for her to snuggle up in. We haven't washed the robe in the hope that it still smells like him. It doesn't to us, but a cat's sense of smell is fourteen times better than a human's, so maybe.

The worst thing in Ting's life these days is her nemesis, the kamikaze cardinal—a mama bird who relentlessly dive-bombs the big window by Ting's sunroom ledge. We can't determine whether she's taunting Ting or whether she's going after her own reflection but, regardless, Ting will not be happy until that bird is a snack. We've done everything we can think of to dissuade the cardinal, and the only thing that has worked even a little bit is to hang silver Christmas ribbon from the top of the window to kind of scare her away—a tip we got from our neighbor, Lyn, who got it from the Audubon Society.

Even before her surgery, Ting was showing signs of asthma—loud, raspy coughing fits—and Dr. Belden officially diagnosed her with it about two years ago when Mom and I brought her in to be checked after Googling "feline asthma" and coming up with a video of a black cat having the same kind of attacks as Ting.

At first we just tried getting rid of her (very dusty) scratching post and changing her to a cat litter with less dust—even tried litter made from corn cobs instead of clay. Those things helped a bit, perhaps, but not enough. Then, thinking it might be a bacterial lung infection, Dr. Belden prescribed the antibiotic Clavamox. It didn't really do the trick either. So now, to lessen the frequency and severity of the attacks, we give Ting two different medications via inhaler twice a day each: a red one (albuterol) and an orange one (Flovent).

As with the pacemaker, they don't make special asthma medication for cats, so she uses meds made for humans that we buy at our local drugstore. Both come with counters so that we know how many puffs are left. We administer each dose using a device called an AeroKat—a plastic cylinder about the size of a small water bottle, with a soft rubber face mask at one end and a place to attach the inhaler at the other. Close to the top of the AeroKat there's a little green lever that moves up and down as Ting breathes. The trick is to press the inhaler exactly when she's breathing in so that the medicine gets deep into her lungs. It sounds easy, and it is—unless, of course, she's squirming. On the whole, though, she doesn't seem to mind it; she just looks at us each time we approach her, chamber in hand, as if to say *Again?*

The medicine definitely helps, but Ting still has a half-dozen mild asthma attacks most days, depending on the weather and the pollen count. Although each attack will eventually stop on its own (usually within a minute), we've learned that there are things we can do to comfort her and shorten them. So, when she has one, we pick her up and sort of burp her like a baby, or stand her on her hind legs and raise her front paws over her head to stretch her body, or scratch her neck in a downward motion or her chest in an upward one, or offer her a drink of water. One of these approaches has always worked so far, but we have an emergency inhaler handy, just in case. And, if her asthma gets worse, there's a pill we can start to give her. Dr. Belden has already written the prescription.

The one downside of the asthma medication is that it makes Ting's ears paper thin. Consequently, the tips fold over when she sleeps. Fixing them is like trying to separate two rose petals that have gotten stuck together. We start each morning gently rolling out her ears, bringing them back to their full, upright, and locked position. She usually purrs while we do it, happy to have us making a fuss.

We've also started feeding her human baby food. About a year ago she stopped eating the dry cat food on which she grew up, and started losing weight. Dr. Belden feared her appetite was off because her kidney function was declining—a common problem in older cats—and advised us to try to switch her from dry food to wet, in an effort to maximize her fluid intake. We tried everything—from the good stuff (Iams, Eukanuba, Science Diet, Blue Buffalo) to the naughty (Friskies, Whiskas, etc.). After learning they were owned by Mars—the same company that makes Milky Way and Snickers (who wouldn't want a Milky Way, right?)— I went out and bought some Sheba, including their Premium Cuts variety pack, which, I kid you not, had a Korat on the box. But the Sheba was a no-go.

You name the brand, we gave it a try, in every available flavor—from beef to turkey, shrimp to rabbit, lamb to liver, cod to tilapia. We tried minced, sliced, and flaked; we tried grilled, we tried roasted. We tried one with "chunky chopped marinated morsels" that we could barely get out of the can. We tried a pâté with aged cheddar that looked so good I was tempted to put it on a Triscuit and eat it myself. We tried vegetarian and Mediterranean, and if we could have found it, we'd have tried Rastafarian. (Speaking of which, I started wondering if we should investigate medical marijuana for Ting after seeing a CBS News report on how it increased the appetite of cancer patients;

wasn't sure how we'd get her to smoke it, though.) We tried vegan, organic, and organic vegan. We tried a kosher kind called Evanger's, which sounded vaguely evangelical to me, which didn't make much sense. We even tried the Fancy Feast Elegant Medleys—the names of which made my own mouth water (Chicken Tuscany with Long Grain Rice, Tuna Primavera with Garden Veggies, and the oh-so-enticing Turkey Florentine)—as well as the Fancy Feast gourmet breakfasts, including the *really* fancy-sounding Soufflé with Wild Salmon.

If we could've gotten Ting to eat any of it, she would have been eating better than I do. But of course she refused it all—wouldn't give it a sniff, much less a lick. Exasperated, we e-mailed Dr. Belden, who promptly suggested we try Beech-Nut or Gerber baby food. Duh. Everything else that had helped her so far had been human—pacemaker, asthma medicine, and so on. Why shouldn't it be the same with food?

It took a week and several trips to the market, but we finally found a flavor Ting really liked—Gerber Chicken and Gravy. Months later, by accident (the jars look alike), we found a second flavor that passed muster—Gerber Turkey and Gravy. The moral of the story: She may be from Thailand, but, like any good American, our cat likes gravy.

Feeding Ting baby food is actually quite the process. It begins with recognizing the signs she's hungry: a pleading

look, followed by an insistent meow that could charitably be described as a bleating lamb, but more accurately described as a squeezed gnome. That's our cue to lean down to her and ask, "Do you want baby food?" She almost always answers, and her answer is almost always yes. So we raise a finger in front of her face and say "One minute."

Then it's off to the refrigerator to get the jar of baby food, because Ting refuses to eat it if it's at room temperature. She also refuses to eat it off a plate, or a dish, or even a silver spoon. So, after walking upstairs while tapping the spoon on the jar lid three times and singing the words *bay bee food* (we have no idea how this came to be part of the process, but it's been that way for months), we use the spoon to scoop a blob of the gelatinous stuff into our palm, and then kneel down to her and hold out our hand until she starts to eat from it. Or not.

When it comes to Ting and baby food, it's a crapshoot. She usually doesn't eat it if it's from a new jar—the flavor is just too strong. But a jar that has been open in the fridge for a couple of days is, to her, absolutely perfect. The only trick is to stay still long enough for Ting to get her fill, because if you move or, God forbid, talk, she'll stop eating. It's hard not to laugh when she nears the end of her meal and her tongue starts to tickle your palm. And, of course, we have to be careful not to let the baby food slip through the space between our fingers, which just makes an ungodly mess on the floor—one that Ting has absolutely no interest in help-ing to clean up.

On an average day, we can get almost a full jar of baby food in Ting, but because she'll only eat a spoonful at a time, and because she'll only eat in Mom's bedroom, it means we have to go up and down the stairs at least a dozen times. Because I work, Mom bears the brunt. I came home one night to find that she had bought a little fridge like the one I had in my college dorm room, put it in her bedroom, and stocked it with jars of baby food.

In addition to being Ting's waitress, sometimes Mom is Ting's chef. Ting will eat chicken that Mom bakes for her, so long as she lets it cool completely before cutting it into tiny pieces and serving it to Ting. Ting will eat the chicken off a plate—but not a paper plate (they slide around too much); it has to be a ceramic plate. Still, at least we don't have to palm it like we do the baby food.

Ting will also eat Temptations treats—the yellow-fin tuna or free-range chicken kind from their Naturals line, which has no artificial flavors, but does have added miner-als like taurine, which is good for the heart muscle.

And of course, Ting still drinks from a people glass. Because her fluid intake matters now more than ever due to the threat of kidney failure, we often bring the glass over to where she's sitting and hold it for her while she drinks—even in the middle of the night. Dr. Belden also suggested that we start giving Ting subcutaneous injections of fluid every two or three days, and showed us how to do it. It requires a ridiculous amount of choreography—so much so that I think of it as ballet with needles.

First, one of us (usually me) has to distract Ting while the other gets out the IV bag. If it's a new bag, there's a rubber stopper to be removed from the giving port and a plastic spike to be inserted—carefully, so as not to puncture the bag from the inside. Then one of us (usually Mom) warms the bag in a pot of hot water in the sink so that the fluid's not cold when we give it to Ting. Once she judges the bag to be warm enough by holding it to her cheek, she attaches a needle to the end of the line and twists off the cap before loosening the pinch clamp and moving the wheel clamp to the open position, to start the fluid flowing. She lets it go for a few seconds so that the fluid in the line is sure to be warm.

Meanwhile, I'm upstairs with Ting, trying not to let her see me take out the hot-pink bath mat on which we position her to give her the injection—trying not to let her see me tear open a gauze pad and place it on the floor, still in its sterile wrapper, an arm's length from the mat. We put the mat next to the bedroom door because the light is good there, and because we need to be able to hang the IV bag from a high place so that the fluid flows quickly.

When I hear Mom's footsteps, I pick Ting up and set her on the mat while Mom hooks the bag on the sturdy plastic hanger we keep on the door for just that purpose. Mom kneels on the floor behind Ting and I kneel in front of her, stroking her behind the ears while Mom gathers the scruff behind her neck, takes a deep breath, and inserts the needle. Sometimes it goes in easy, and all I have to do is open the wheel clamp full-throttle and let the solution flow right into her for about two minutes. That's all it takes to give her the full dose. It's my job to close the clamp when we're done, remove the needle from Ting while Mom holds her, and apply the gauze pad with a bit of pressure so that there's no leakage from the injection site. Two or three times I forgot to close the clamp first, and poor little Ting got a bit of a bath.

If the needle goes in hard, it's a whole different story. It means the flow will be slow because the needle is up against tissue, and Ting probably won't stay still long enough to get the full dose. When this happens, we try to distract her with kisses and scratches, but usually end up having to content ourselves with half a dose. We make up for it by giving her the next subQ in two days rather than three.

Occasionally the needle goes in *too* easy—right through the other side of the scruff. Because the area is covered in fur, we usually can't tell until we start the drip and see a little puddle start to form between Ting's shoulder blades. It means we have to take the needle out and try again. And it means Ting will be upset with us, because what cat likes getting wet? And who wants to be stabbed not once, but twice? I know from all my own needle-play that it's unpleasant while it's happening and not unusual to be sore afterward. Still, she needs her injections, just as I need mine.

Between the hand-delivered water, the subQ injections, and good old Gerber, we manage to get enough fluid into Ting to keep her fully hydrated and feeling good.

Ting is the only one for whom I buy baby food. I'm forty-two now. I still want to have a child, but I know the percentages are against me and, if I want to get pregnant, it may be something of a science experiment. To further complicate matters, Copaxone is a pregnancy category B medication—meaning while animal studies haven't shown adverse effects, no formal studies have yet been done with pregnant women. Dr. Weiner said the best course of action would be to conceive, then go right off the Copaxone. Apparently pregnant women don't get new lesions; the pregnancy offers protection from flares.

Even though I could potentially carry a child to term, sometimes I think about adopting. When I worry I wouldn't love a child I adopted as much as one to whom I gave birth, I think of Ting and how much I love her, and I know I could.

I know, too, that I won't always have Ting. When I lose her, I will mourn her like I've mourned all the other people I've lost—like I mourned my grandmother, my grandfather, and my dad; like I mourned Cinnamon, the cat who came before her. I will tell complete strangers all about her, and I won't stop talking even when they've stopped listening. I will not adopt another cat—except, of course, I will.

My dad's clothes still hang in his closet. His shoes still line the closet floor. When we need an envelope, we still go to the drawer where he kept them, with his tape dispenser and his magnifying glass. When we need to ready paperwork for filing, we still use his old-fashioned silver stapler. And we still look things up in his Rolodex—the address for the bank where we have a safety deposit box; the phone number for the car repair place where the owner was his friend.

The thing no one tells you about grief is that it's permanent. I've heard people talk about "picking up the pieces" after someone you love dies, but I see no evidence that it's possible. You learn to step over the pieces, I suppose. But the pieces are always there.

My father's birthday is still the first thing I mark whenever I buy a new calendar. I still think about him every day. The littlest things remind me—filling my car at the gas station where he used to buy lottery tickets; standing next to a man on the subway whose aftershave is a bit like the Aramis that Dad always wore (and that Ting so often smelled like); seeing rugelach in a bakery case; an ad for matzo ball soup, or brisket, or bagels and lox, or hot pastrami. When I get a letter with a pretty stamp—especially a foreign one—I still cut around it and tuck it in his old cigar box, just like I did when he was alive, because he used to collect them. But I can finally fall asleep without the TV on. I'm being called from the dugout. There's a chance I'll save the game.

The good luck cat continues to have good luck. We take Ting to Angell for a pacemaker interrogation—a test to see if it's functioning properly, and to measure the battery life. As always, Sara comes to the lobby and shows us into the exam room. After she takes Ting's weight and makes notes on how she's doing, we have time to chat with her before Dr. Laste arrives. She has news: She's going to be starting veterinary school. We'll miss her, but we're terribly proud of her. We know she'll help generations of animals.

When Dr. Laste arrives she gently feels around Ting's pacemaker. It's still going strong, but has migrated a bit, probably due to all of the times she has jumped off the bed or the couch. It's still in the same general area, though, and Ting still seems completely unaware of it. Dr. Laste listens to her heart with a stethoscope, and looks pleased.

Then she ushers us into the room next door, where we're soon joined by a representative from the pacemaker company, who has been part of Ting's team since the beginning. She places a wand-like object attached to a computer against Ting's pacemaker while I hold her in my arms. With it, they're able to determine how often Ting is using the pacemaker, and recalibrate it accordingly so that it fires only when truly necessary, thus saving the battery as much as possible. After some calculation, Dr. Laste turns to us and says Ting is barely using the device.

I guess her heart just needed time to heal.

ACKNOWLEDGMENTS

There are no words to express my gratitude to cardiologist Dr. Nancy Laste at Angell Animal Medical Center, and to our longtime vet, Dr. Karen Belden, at Bulger Veterinary Hospital. If it weren't for the two of you, my family would be smaller. Thank you for saving Ting. May every animal in this world have people like you to help them.

To my agent, Peter Rubie, at Fine Print Literary Management, and my editor, Keith Wallman: You've been good to me for two books now, and I'm grateful for you both. Thanks for your advocacy on my behalf, and for your always-wise counsel.

To the people I work with at Da Capo Press: Thank you for being such collegial colleagues, and for the support you've shown me over the years. It never once occurred to me that I should hide my MS at work. That speaks volumes.

Even though he's no longer here to read this, I want, of course, to acknowledge my dad. To quote a song we used to sing together while driving in the car, "The story that I love you, it has no end."

To my mom, who fights for me like no other, and who fought for Dad until the end. Thank you for nursing Ting back to health in the way that only a mother could.

And to Marc, in sickness and in health—regardless of the paperwork.

ABOUT THE AUTHOR

Lissa Warren is vice president, senior director of publicity, and acquiring editor at Da Capo Press. The author of *The Savvy Author's Guide to Book Publicity*, she holds a BS in English education from Miami University and an MFA in creative writing from Bennington College. Her poetry has appeared in *Quarterly West*, *Oxford Magazine*, *Black Warrior Review*, and *Verse*, and she serves as a poetry editor for *Post Road*. She also serves on the advisory council of Southern New Hampshire University's MFA writing program. Since 2003, she has been an adjunct professor at Boston's Emerson College, teaching graduate courses in book editing, book publicity, and book publishing as part of its Writing, Literature, and Publishing program. She lives in southern New Hampshire.